MW00456259

The Messy MARKETPLACE

Selling Your Business in a World of Imperfect Buyers

BRENT BESHORE

The Messy Marketplace
Selling Your Business in a World of Imperfect Buyers

ISBN   978-0-9980300-0-5 (hardcover)
          978-0-9980300-1-2 (ebook)

Published by:
Boring Books

A NOTE FROM THE AUTHOR

My name is Brent Beshore and I'm the founder and CEO of adventur.es, a firm that invests in and partners with closely-held, family-operated companies in North America.

If you're reading this, you're likely an entrepreneur, the family member or close friend of a business owner, or an advisor to an owner. While no one likes to admit it, the unavoidable truth is, at some point, in some way, each business must be transitioned — years pass, people age, markets change. This often carries an unfortunate amount of stress, anxiety, and frustration. Most of the time, transitioning is a once-in-a-lifetime occurrence and the traditional paths are unnecessarily opaque.

Do something enough and you get good at it. Just as you have built your expertise, over more than a decade, my colleagues and I have had the privilege to peek behind the curtain at over 10,000 companies — reviewing financial statements, meeting with leadership, and seeking to understand what makes each company tick. We are professional investors, and this is what we do day in and day out.

Talking with hundreds of business owners, we noticed that many of the same questions, concerns, and thoughts repeat. And that makes sense. Just as all businesses share many commonalities, sellers of those businesses will have mostly similar experiences, with differences in personality, motivation, and situation driving the nuance.

This book attempts to demystify transacting from a seller's point of view. As much as the finance industry likes to pretend to be "buttoned up," they're largely disorganized and unnecessarily shrouded in mystery. The title says it all—it's a messy marketplace, with every type, temperament, and motive imaginable.

The goal of this book is to help sellers, the families of sellers, sellers' advisors, and company leadership to understand the market for smaller companies, allowing them to make better decisions and create better outcomes.

Our hope is that you walk away from this book better prepared to understand the path forward, the vantage points of everyone involved, and the process of a transition through a transaction with an outside investor. Whether you choose this course or another, such as an employee stock ownership plan or a management buyout, being informed is the best path towards making that choice responsibly.

There is no pitch for my firm in these pages. That said, if I, or anyone at adventur.es, can be of assistance, please don't hesitate to reach out. You can find our contact information at www.adventur.es.

Cheers,
Brent

CONTENTS

Behind the Curtain:

These appendices provide information that, in-process, will likely be sourced from your advisors and prospective buyer(s).

THE SITUATION

You own a business. Perhaps you founded it. Perhaps your grandfather and great-aunt did. Regardless of origin, the business has been a driving force in your life for decades.

At some point, your business became a "company." By that I mean your business employs lots of people, has considerable revenue, and, by all measures, has achieved success. It's not a fledgling startup finding its way. It's not a distressed organization that has lost its way. It's not a portfolio of real estate holdings, or a pile of assets. It's a community of people you brought together to accomplish difficult, valuable things on behalf of your customers.

At the same time, your business is not a "corporation." The business is privately owned by you, or a handful of people, not publicly traded. If you have a board of directors, it's likely made up of the company's leaders. You don't have an acquisitions team. Your business is operating in your area of expertise, generating roughly $1 million to $15 million in annual pre-tax net profits.

While you've kept your head down in the business, time has passed. Perhaps your spouse is telling you it's time to step back professionally and travel more. Perhaps the company has scaled to a size you feel ill-suited to lead. Perhaps your doctor is telling you it's time to slow down. Perhaps you merely feel ready to pass the torch.

Whatever the reason, you're beginning to consider if, how, and when to sell. And whether to sell all or only a part of your company.

This book is a reference guide to your unanswered questions about the messy marketplace of imperfect buyers. It's about the realities of selling your company. It's about the emotional peaks and valleys, the sleepless nights, and the hurdles you have to overcome.

There are no quick tricks or silver bullets within these pages. It won't replace hiring competent advisors. It won't help you "sell for a crazy price."

The objectives of this book are to shine light on unfamiliar aspects of selling, help you avoid common pitfalls, and provide a fuller picture of the circumstances, process, and people involved in private company transactions.

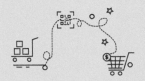

PREP:
Considerations Around Selling

Like most aspects of business, the decision to sell is complicated. I've never heard of a business owner waking up one day with the epiphany: "I should sell my business!" It's an ongoing process of discovery. This section helps you evaluate if you're ready, and the preparation required to enter the marketplace confidently.

CONTENTS:
- Setting The Goal
- Emotional Encounters
- Rumor Has It
- Deal Killers
- It's All Confidential
- Big News

Setting The Goal

Why do you want to sell?
What do you hope to get out of it?

These simple questions broach a complicated topic. As an entrepreneur myself, I understand how motivations, opportunity costs, and life circumstances change. Through the years, I've swung between elation after a big win to depression after a major loss. My levels of motivation have fluctuated between tap dancing to work and forcing myself out of bed. I've thought my business was going to print money, and I've contemplated bankruptcy. Entrepreneurship offers the highest of highs and the lowest of lows.

Ultimately, we all must sell, pass along, or shut down our companies. The only alternative is to roll the dice by doing nothing. Upon your eventual passing, or incapacitation, your family will be left to clean up the mess. The company will be rudderless, and the best customers and employees will jump ship. All too often, decisions left to the next generation create infighting amongst heirs over who gets what, and when. The financial needs of the family can be stretched thin, creating increased stress and pressure. It's a recipe for disaster.

If you choose a proactive path to selling, the next set of questions to address are: *When? To whom? For how much, and under what circumstances?*

Both buyers and sellers have ever-changing needs, desires, and options. As a seller you should have an understanding of the landscape prior to heading down a path to transition, and work, over time, to assemble the necessary ingredients for a successful transaction.

There are seven root motivations for transitioning a company: personality/skills, exhaustion, freedom, health, obligations, risk, and legacy. Notice, I didn't mention money. That's because you'll almost always do better financially, assuming the company continues to

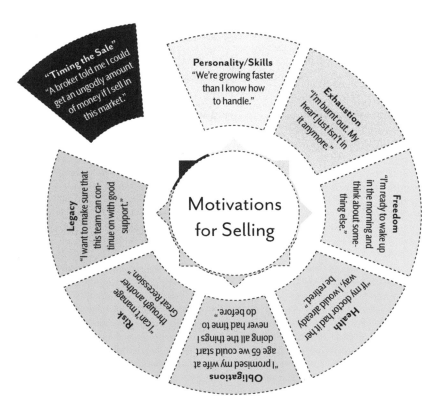

Motivations for Selling

- "Timing the Sale" — "A broker told me I could get an ungodly amount of money if I sell in this market."
- **Personality/Skills** — "We're growing faster than I know how to handle."
- **Exhaustion** — "I'm burnt out. My heart just isn't in it anymore."
- **Freedom** — "I'm ready to wake up in the morning and think about something else."
- **Health** — "If my doctor had it her way, I would already be retired."
- **Obligations** — "I promised my wife at age 65 we could start doing all the things I never had time to do before."
- **Risk** — "I can't manage through another Great Recession."
- **Legacy** — "I want to make sure that this team can continue on with good support."

perform, by <u>not</u> selling your company. It's counterintuitive, but correct. Except on very rare occasions, your lifetime earnings potential will decrease as the result of a sale, because the investments you make with sale proceeds will likely never measure up to the fruits of running your own company. It's always more profitable to leverage your financial resources against your time, wisdom, and relationships in your area of expertise.

But before diving in, I want to hit on an eighth motivation that can be seductive, but is ultimately fool's gold—"timing" the sale. Some sellers think they're going to "pull one over" on a buyer, and some do. They try to "top-tick" the cyclicality of their industry, or sell out

5

Selling Vs. Maintaining Ownership

HYPOTHETICAL SITUATION: You own a strong, relatively stable manufacturing company that is currently producing $5 million per year in owner earnings after capital expenditures.

SELL: You agree to an offer that includes $15 million in cash at close + $10 million in a seller note after 5 years at 5% interest.

Total Proceeds Over 5 Years:
$27,500,000

OWN: You find a great executive to lead the company, allowing you to take a few steps back, and the company continues to grow, averaging 5% per year.

Total Earnings Over 5 Years:
$27,628,156.25 +
The Value of the Business

Beyond the basic math, you must contemplate tax consequences, risk tolerance and more.

Of course, there are lots of ways these scenarios can go sideways, or in better directions. The point is that when you sell, your timeline to earn proceeds from the company becomes finite, thus limiting your earnings potential.

of what they know will be a dire situation. I'd caution against that way of thinking. It will be obvious and you'll select for a group of buyers that will likely create challenges for you and your employees. As Warren Buffett's long-time business partner Charlie Munger once said, "How do you get a good spouse? Deserve it." I'd suggest the same. Be a seller that attracts a great buyer.

The first motivation I call the entrepreneurial conundrum. Most entrepreneurs are strong-willed, contrarian control freaks. Believe me, I am one. Those personality traits are essential for launching a company and sustaining it through periods of tumult. Without your sheer force of will, your company wouldn't have made it to where it is today. But what got you here won't get you there. The same character traits that made you successful are holding the team back and you know you need to bring in leadership that can fulfill the company's potential.

Next are a grouping of motivations that are straightforward: exhaustion, freedom, health, and obligations. Many sellers are simply exhausted, and for good reason. Operating a company can be a grind. It's stressful and all-consuming. Health, family obligations, and life circumstances may all be driving forces in your decision. Or perhaps you just want the time to pursue a passion, hobby, or alternative career. One person who sold a company to my firm is now a professional artist, realizing a lifelong dream.

When it comes to "risk," every owner can relate, although each situation is unique. It's a negative surprise, and potentially one that can have long-term ramifications. The 2008 financial crisis exposed the depth and breadth of potential outcomes. Roughly a decade later, I heard frequently from sellers who were still recovering, and many more who will never get back what they lost. It's tragic. A perfectly good reason to sell is out of concern for risk. If you've run a successful company, chances are that you've made a good bit of money already, but not enough for lifelong comfort. Selling all, or a portion, of your company is a great way to de-risk.

There's also legacy. I suspect that as you've become financially successful, the money means less and your legacy means more. You want to put your company in good hands. You want your employees and co-workers treated well and with respect. You want your reputation to remain intact. You want to ensure you can retire without being a burden on family members, and you possibly want to provide for those family members and causes important to you. How your community, colleagues, friends, and family remember you will depend on the choices you make in transitioning your business.

Regardless of your motivations, it's important to think about what outcomes are important and why. Here's a cheat sheet:

I want between $_____ and
$_____ of cash as a financial result of the transac-
tion. (Remember, you'll have to pay off debt, taxes, and transaction
costs. Also, something is only worth what someone is willing to
pay for it.)

I want to work for _____ years in my current
position, and am willing to consult with the company
for _____ years thereafter. (It's okay to say you want to die in
your office chair, or leave the day of closing.)

I'm looking for a buyer/partner that will take
the _____ role in the company. (Example roles
include advisory board, passive partner, CEO, and CFO.)

The characteristics/values of an ideal buyer would be:

My ideal timeline for a transaction would be _____ , but I'd be
happy to sell in _____ years.

My top non-financial goals are:

Answering these questions is the foundation for creating a pur-
poseful path. In all likelihood, you won't be able to complete all of
these sentences right now. If you can address all of them already,
you're way ahead of most sellers, but may have left some options
unexplored. Now for a few warnings...

Emotional Encounters

All the stakeholders in a transaction are human, and all humans are messy, emotional creatures. My experience is that expectations and the management of emotions play a crucial role in every deal.

To start with you, the seller, a transaction is going to be an emotionally challenging and draining process. Expect nothing less. I've never heard of a deal going "smoothly." Anything worth doing is going to be hard, and selling your company is no exception.

You're going to have moments of doubt, feelings of losing control, and misaligned expectations. You will get confusing signals and receive conflicting advice. The pace will always be too fast, except when it's too slow. You will encounter unexpected and unpredictable situations.

You need to prepare mentally for a grueling experience. If the formula for happiness is reality minus expectations, start lowering your expectations. There is no perfect buyer, no perfect lawyer, no perfect intermediary, and no perfect seller, you included.

Once you are comfortable that you can handle the strain, consider those stakeholders with less control in the process—your family and your employees. Each carry their own set of fears, hopes, baggage, and expectations.

Your employees will naturally distrust and fear any transaction. Everyone has heard horror stories. The cliche, "Nothing will change after the merger," is always a load of crap. Of course, things will change, and employees know it. The only questions are how, when, and how much change will occur. Most employees expect buyers will "synergize" cost out of the business. Put more frankly, they assume the new owner will fire people, because most professional buyers do exactly that. Employees will want reassurance that their jobs are safe and their roles will remain intact.

Family dynamics are always unique, and odd things tend to happen when large sums of money are at stake. I'd highly suggest talking with your significant other, children, or close relatives prior to a transaction, or immediately thereafter. Everyone will be curious and it's better to tackle the tough stuff upfront. What are you planning to do with the money? How will your role, time constraints, and obligations change as a result of the transaction?

Rumor Has It

If you're a private person, you likely haven't told many people about your intent to sell. In truth, if you own a private company, selling is a private process and it's nobody's business apart from the participating parties. But you've likely still heard stories about other people's experiences.

Behavioral psychologists have spent years researching why some bits of information and stories are volunteered and frequently shared. In general, bad news travels faster and further. The more outlandish the tale, the greater the entertainment value. This is why so many good companies have passionate negative reviews written about them, while the positive stories are brief (if they exist at all).

The same behaviors hold true for the rumor mill around selling a private business. Emotions run high during the process. If someone has an inordinately bad experience, others are likely to hear about it. Rumors are shared more often than facts.

As I've gotten to know owners through the process of evaluating their businesses, I have heard some doozies. A seller with a limited frame of reference considers the story they heard to be the rule, rather than the exception, and, as a prospective buyer, my job becomes explaining the likelihood of such a situation in deals with us.

The rumor mill tends to exaggerate, of course, but an element of truth is usually embedded. Here are some of the most common rumors I hear from concerned sellers, and context for thinking through them:

The only cash you'll get is the cash at close.

Later in the book, we'll discuss payment structures used in transactions. In general, most deals allocate a percentage of proceeds to be delivered in the years following the sale. There are horror stories of buyers finding ways to manipulate situations so that the sellers do not receive money owed to them in future years. However rare, these situations serve as a good lesson on why the integrity and proven track record of a buyer can be as important as the size of their checkbook.

All buyers are created equal.

Selling an operating business is not like selling a car or a piece of real estate. The sale price is important, but not nearly the full picture. There's tremendous nuance to how the price gets paid, under what circumstances, and over what period of time, as well as what happens to all the stakeholders post-close. The buyer will greatly influence the outcome, which means the integrity, work ethic, and style of the buyer matters tremendously.

Most of your people will be fired.

In general, most employees won't be fired. Unless your firm is obviously bloated and disorganized, it makes little sense for a buyer to arbitrarily fire people. Finding and retaining talent is a key risk to all businesses and professional buyers know this.

There are two dominant reasons a buyer will let go of staff post-close, redundancy and efficiency, both of which should be obvious before closing. When sold to a larger corporation and, where there is overlap in positions and responsibilities, the corporate employees usually win out. And, the traditional private equity playbook is to remove as much cost as possible from overhead. It's a lot easier to boost the bottom line short-term through cost cutting than growth.

The other situation is if the business is being sold "for parts." This may be the case if the overall business is not doing well, but houses a valuable division, customer list, or intellectual property. Depending on the team required to make that asset valuable, some or all of your team may be let go post-close.

I encourage you to ask potential buyers detailed questions about their post-close plans.

Your insight and involvement will not be needed/wanted post-close.

For a few buyer types, particularly those who intend to install leadership and have a business plan or formula for how the company will operate moving forward, your transition may be short and require relatively little involvement on your part. However, even if you do not continue full-time with the company, most buyers will want your insight and participation over a period of at least one to five years, depending on the complexity of the business and layers of leadership remaining. Either way, the intent of the buyer should be clear in their offer, which will include the amount of time they expect you to remain with the company post-close, specific responsibilities, and what involvement, if any, they want you to have after the transition is complete.

Tell buyers what they want to hear. That's how you get the best valuation.

A frustrating part of the process for buyers can be reconciling how a company is marketed with what is discovered during due diligence. Hiding flaws or skewing the presentation of numbers will only delay the inevitable. And if they discover things previously undisclosed or spun in a disingenuous way, the buyer will re-negotiate the deal, or walk away altogether. If you start with the truth, warts and all, the odds of success rise dramatically. More on this in the next section.

Deal Killers

Before you start going down the path toward a transaction, I'd highly suggest you take an honest look at major weaknesses of current operations and any skeletons in the closet. Most businesses have issues, and they can almost always be addressed. The buyer will figure them out eventually, and usually after you've both exhausted considerable resources. The best way to handle hard truths is head-on and early in the process.

Here are a few of the challenging situations I've experienced with sellers:

Management Killers

OWNER RELIANCE: The biggest issue most businesses face is reliance on ownership. The owner holds the top relationships, leads strategy, makes the investment decisions, and holds the bulk of the expertise. The more reliant on ownership, the lower the purchase price and likelihood of sale. Leadership development and systems-building should be a focus for anyone looking to exit.

EXECUTIVE TURNOVER: Buyers want stability and a driving force of that is the leadership. If you've experienced high levels of executive turnover, it may prove a challenging component of the sale process.

Operations Killers

CONCENTRATION: As the adage goes, don't put all your eggs in one basket. The more concentrated the customer or supplier base, the more dependent your company is on someone else's success. Selling a business with significant concentration is not impossible, but you must be able to get the buyer comfortable with the risk.

CUSTOMER INSTABILITY: Customer satisfaction is paramount, especially if you have a concentrated customer base. If there have been challenges with losing major clients or elevated customer turnover, I'd recommend putting together case studies that show why it happened and why it's unlikely to happen again.

WARRANTY ISSUES: All products have some warranty claims, but extreme cases can be a real problem. They raise questions about the design process, product quality, and long-term liability associated with the business. Be sure to clearly explain warranty liabilities and help the buyer understand the risk profile, which is almost always nuanced.

Financial Killers

LIENS: Liens create uncertainty. If someone claims your company owes a significant debt, whether it's to Uncle Sam or another business, they don't go away just because the company is sold. Disclose any liens and work towards getting them resolved. The more people who need to check off on a transaction, the higher the likelihood of failure.

CREATIVE TAX STRATEGIES: One of the advantages of owning a business is being able to write off part of your life as an expense benefiting the company. Everyone does it, but there are some lines that will make a buyer uncomfortable. I'd suggest a frank conversation with your tax attorney or CPA about how a buyer would assess your expense allocation in the business. If the transaction is going to be in stock, then the buyer will inherit that liability, which is something I'll discuss later.

OFF-THE-BOOKS: Some owners choose to make certain transactions "off-the-books," meaning they are not recorded properly for a variety of purposes. If you're doing this, stop. No reputable buyer is going to be comfortable with suppliers being paid in cash, or your bookie being employed as a consultant (true story).

Legal Killers

LITIGATION: Ongoing litigation, recurring litigation, or the threat of either, creates a challenging sale environment, mostly because of uncertainty. If the sum is small, consider settling the matter. The buyer is not going to be keen on getting mired in a legal battle.

CONTRACTORS VS. EMPLOYEES: Professional buyers are particularly sensitive to risks associated with employee classification, which can be costly and persistent. If there's any question about the legality of your employee arrangements, have a professional check it out and follow their recommendations.

Non-Business Killers

PERSONAL DYNAMICS: Buyers are people, too. We know life is messy and people make mistakes. Most buyers will move beyond almost anything if you proactively disclose and explain. We've seen deals fall apart because of threatened divorces, ex-spouses' unofficial influence, and not-so-silent "silent" debt holders. Bankruptcies, arrests/convictions, past tax liens, and semi-public problems should be handled transparently and disclosed upon entering due diligence.

It's All Confidential

Prospective buyers will ask you some of the most challenging and personal questions you've encountered. It's important to answer honestly. You don't have to bare your soul, but being overly vague or refusing to talk about yourself and your accomplishments will likely stall progress. The information you share with them will remain confidential.

In spite of the rumors, almost all private sale information remains private. Professional investors' reputations depend on their discretion. If they are not trustworthy, no one will share another opportunity with them. But if someone is inexperienced, I'd recommend having a conversation around confidentiality.

All encounters with prospective investors of mature businesses generally begin with a simple non-disclosure agreement, and this should serve as the symbol of the confidential nature of the discussion for all parties involved. Once this is signed, be prepared and willing to share details. Reputable investors are not going to pump you for information and then steal it to replicate your business.

Big News

As you start down the path to a sale, it's important that you're thoughtful about when and how to discuss the process and likely outcome with each stakeholder. If there's an unexpected area where I see people stumble, this is it. Information is either needlessly offered and becomes a distraction, or is unnecessarily withheld and creates confusion and frustration.

One of the scariest words in the English language is "change." You'll have bouts of anxiety in the process and you're in control. Now put yourself in the shoes of passive participants. Their lives will change without any control. It's important that you spend time mentally walking in their shoes. Keep their emotional reactions in perspective, because they won't always be what you expect.

SIGNIFICANT OTHER: As your life-partner, your significant other will play a key role in the transaction. That may be surprising, but I've never seen a transaction where it didn't happen. They will offer emotional support, be a sounding board and a "gut check," and ultimately cheer you across the finish line. Remember, it's going to be a grueling process and you'll need people to lean on confidentially. Have conversations with them early on to discuss your motivations. As time passes, they can help remind you of your reasons for selling. This will come in handy when negotiations get stressful and the process drags on, which it will.

Leadership Team

There's no way to consummate a transaction without participation from your leadership team. The questions are: who to involve, at what level, and when? If the day-to-day operations of your company are run by someone else, I'd highly advise you have a frank and transparent discussion with that person at the beginning of the process. You should set low expectations around timeline and keep them regularly updated on the transaction progress.

The most senior financial employee is crucial. As explained later in detail, there will be a tremendous amount of information to be gathered, sorted, and examined. The more you, as the owner, are personally gathering the information, the more suspicious a buyer will be of your involvement. The buyer wants to see that the company's leadership can stand on their own and will often use due diligence to test prospective future employees.

Beyond the day-to-day operator and financial leader, the degree of involvement on your team is largely situation-driven. Understand that senior team members who are not included, or included late in the process, will make deductions based on that fact. They'll assume they're not as important, trustworthy, or competent as those included. Keeping the circle of those "in the know" small may be worth the cost, but it can get challenging.

On the contrary, the more people who know, the more likely word will get out in an uncontrolled manner. You should have a very firm "loose lips sink ships" discussion with each person you involve in the process. While confidentiality may be obvious to you, it's not always apparent to other participants. Remember, the sale of the company will be the "hottest news" in your employees' worlds and is often used as a bargaining chip in office politics. It's unfortunate, but true.

Employees

This is the trickiest stakeholder group. In most cases, I recommend not making a general announcement until a transaction is completed. Even when there is a solid commitment, a deal isn't done until the ink is dry <u>and</u> the check clears. It's important to work closely with the buyer to shape the story and avoid any missteps.

When you make the announcement, the first question each person will immediately think about is, "What does this mean for me?" The normal reaction is anxiety about job security, income, and benefits. Everyone has heard horror stories and most people are highly distrustful of "private equity," usually for good reason.

Tackle the fear head-on. Explain the basis of the transaction in the simplest terms possible, including what it means for employees. It's important that you don't make promises you can't keep. If there are going to be layoffs, a reduction in benefits, or a very different culture superimposed on the company, the worst thing you can do is lie.

A thoughtful buyer should be more than willing to collaboratively craft a truthful, substantive message.

Family

Depending on role, family members are often aware of an impending transaction. In the same way leadership team members will make inferences based on their involvement, so will family members. Keep them in mind if they're not in the loop. Post-close, family members will have questions about what it means financially for you, for them, and how your involvement in the company will change.

Most owners will go through a period of working <u>more</u> after the transaction, <u>not less</u>, which can be counterintuitive and confusing. You likely have decades of institutional knowledge to sift through and transfer to the new ownership. And, depending on your post-close role, you may still have day-to-day responsibilities to your team. The first year in transition is always challenging, with trust being established and miscommunication happening often. It requires an extraordinary amount of time to transition well. Rest assured it won't go on forever, but prepare your family that it's not a "get the money and run" situation.

Customers

Most buyers will want to talk with at least a handful of current customers as part of due diligence. Understandably, the customers will be nervous about how their products and services will change after the potential transaction. It's important that you pick the right customers and communicate clearly.

Industry

You likely have deep relationships in your industry and word will get out quickly. Make a list of your relationships and create tiers. The top tier should get a personal call from you. The next tier should get a personal email, keeping in mind that there's a very high likelihood the message will get forwarded on. The purpose of communicating with your industry is to preserve relationships, set proper expectations, and squelch any rumors that pop up.

Press

Depending on the stature of your industry and your company's position within it and your community, you might start getting calls from media outlets. As part of the transition, the buyer, seller, and leadership team should get on the same page about public vs. nonpublic information, who is authorized to speak to the press, and the process for approving any press releases.

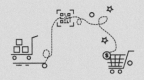

DOING A DEAL:
Selling Your Business

Selling a business isn't like selling, well, anything else. You're selling an "ongoing concern," meaning it's in operation and the dynamics change daily. To further complicate the situation, the marketplace of buyers is fragmented. As such, selling a business is really, really hard, especially if you care who buys it.

CONTENTS:
- Types of Sales
- Types of Buyers
- Role of Advisors
- Financial Structures
- The Negotiation
- Paperwork
- Fees & Costs
- The Process

Types of Sales

As you can imagine, private company transactions come in all flavors, but most fit into two major buckets: majority recapitalization or complete sale. The transaction will be completed as either a stock sale or an asset sale, which have different implications for the buyer and seller.

Selling The Majority vs. Complete Sale

Like every decision, selling 100% of the company's equity comes with advantages and disadvantages. The economics, issues of control, and post-close involvement are usually more straightforward. A complete sale is the best option if the owner wants to get most of the cash up front, have little control post-close, and completely detach from the business within a year, or two. That can sound wonderful, but why wouldn't you want to sell out completely?

To start, you lose upside in the future earnings of the business. You've built the company and know the trajectory better than anyone. If you think the company will continue to prosper, retaining some equity is a great way to get a "second bite of the apple." If the buyer adds significant value to the business, sometimes the retained equity can be worth more than the original stake you sold. It's usually a smaller piece of a bigger pie.

For some quick math, assume a seller retains 20% of the equity. For that stake to be worth more than the original 80% that was sold, the company's value must increase more than 4X. While that sounds daunting, it can happen under the right circumstances and requires around 40% compounding over four years. Growing 40% per year sounds more realistic.

If you choose to roll forward equity and become a minority shareholder, you won't have control, but you will have influence. With some buyers such influence may simply be honorary, maintaining association with the brand and team with little to no involvement in business decisions, while with others it may be more substantive. With skin in the game and a buyer who desires your substantive involvement, you can help shape the company's future, including how it allocates resources, treats employees, and sets strategy. Buyers who welcome substantive involvement do so because it's nearly impossible to replace your background and experience. For others, your prospective ongoing involvement will be difficult — struggle for control, focus, and loyalty — and will therefore be limited in scope.

By law, three general protections are granted to minority shareholders:

1. RIGHT OF INSPECTION: You have the ability to inspect company records that are important to understanding your investment's value.
2. RIGHT TO BRING A DERIVATIVE CLAIM: You can sue the company's board of directors, or officers, if they violate their fiduciary duties, duties of loyalty, or duties of care.
3. RIGHT AGAINST MAJORITY OPPRESSION: The majority shareholder can't reduce a minority shareholder's economic value disproportionately, like giving a larger dividend/distribution than an equity stake warrants.

If you choose to retain equity, it's important to get on the same page as the buyer about how the company will be run and how shareholder relationships will function post-close. As an equity holder, here is a list of questions to discuss with a buyer:

- What are the timeline and expectations for your investment?
- What types of involvement do you want me to have? What happens if we disagree on my level, or type, of involvement?

- If I want to liquidate all or a portion of my remaining shares, may I? Who will buy them, and how do we determine a price?
- If the decision is made to re-sell the company, do I get to choose whether to sell my remaining equity, or not?
- Are there any guarantees you'd expect me to participate in personally?
- As cash is generated from the company's operations, what will be its uses?
- What happens if the business needs more cash to operate? How will capital calls be performed, and under what scenarios?
- How much and what type of debt will be used to complete the transaction, and in the ongoing operations of the company?

Types of Buyers

While all buyers of private businesses are generally lumped together by the term "private equity," there are big differences in who buys companies, the types of investments they make, the control they exert, and their post-close involvement. Different types of buyers buy different types of companies with different levels of involvement. Each type of buyer serves a role in the market, but most can be quickly eliminated from your search based on your goals and the company's situation.

Private Equity Funds

When people say "private equity," they are most commonly referring to a firm that invests pools of capital to make private investments. The General Partners (GPs) collect capital from high net worth individuals and institutions, known as Limited Partners (LPs). The LPs provide the money for a period of time to invest in a specific thesis. Since most funds are structured as ten-year investment vehicles, private equity firms typically spend the first three years making the investments, the next three years holding the investments, and the following few years selling the investments.

This strict schedule has upside and downside for your company and employees. Decisions will necessarily be short-term oriented and focused on generating the highest possible return over that period of time. In fact, the private equity firm has a fiduciary duty to do so. Strategies often include installing new executive leadership, automating processes, expanding product lines, and reducing costs.

Private equity funds are required to invest based on the terms of their funds, which limits the size, industry, and type of company they can acquire. Most groups list their investment criteria publicly to avoid wasting both parties' time on unsuitable opportunities. So, if you are going to consider private equity groups, make sure you meet their investment criteria before reaching out.

Depending on the size of your company and the firm's existing portfolio, your company may be considered a "platform" or an "add-on" (also called a "bolt-on" or "tuck-in" in industry jargon). A platform acquisition is a firm's major investment in a particular sector, which they hope will provide them an organization under which to acquire smaller, similar companies. A bolt-on acquisition is added to an existing platform, sometimes through complete absorption and consolidation, and other times through sharing resources. The earnings before interest, taxes, depreciation and amortization (EBITDA) of a bolt-on may be as small as $500,000, while potential platforms have a minimum of $5 million of EBITDA.

Private equity firms make many more add-on investments than platform investments, and it is important to understand how your company is being considered as a part of their prospective portfolio.

Understanding EBITDA

EBITDA is an acronym that stands for earnings before interest, taxes, depreciation, and amortization, and is commonly used in understanding a company's operating cash flow. Formulaically, it is calculated as:

$$Net\ Income$$
$$+$$
$$Interest$$
$$+$$
$$Taxes$$
$$+$$
$$Depreciation$$
$$+$$
$$Amortization$$
$$=$$
$$EBITDA$$

Most financials prepared for potential buyers go one step further, adding back personal and non-essential expenses to produce "Adjusted EBITDA."

EBITDA is a proxy, but far from a perfect one. All businesses require reinvestment merely to maintain market position. Therefore, EBITDA never represents cash flow to owners. Investors will not accept EBITDA as presented. They will dig into the financials and adjustments to determine the true underlying earnings available to ownership.

Typically, platform acquisitions retain far greater independence and organizational control than add-ons. Get a clear picture of how you, your team, and the brand will be used post-transaction.

Although strategies differ from firm to firm, traditional private equity has developed a reputation for aggressively using debt, often employing financial leverage between 3-6X EBITDA. In the same way a mortgage enables a family to invest in a home with a proportionally small down payment, debt enables private equity groups to write smaller checks. Smaller checks allow a fund to invest in more companies, providing diversification and favorable heads-I-win-tails-you-lose dynamics with non-recourse debt.

This debt creates an urgency amongst company leadership, or, as a private equity friend of mine likes to say, "Debt makes them sweat." Debt is also one of the few ways to put a great company in peril, significantly reducing the margin for error and bad luck. Think about debt as an amplifier. It doesn't change the odds of success, but greatly changes the magnitude. With debt you will make more money if things go right and will lose more money if things go wrong.

Typically, once a private equity fund has owned the company for 2 to 4 years, or the company has grown to a certain size, whichever comes first, the managing partners will seek an exit. Depending on the size and type of company, they may sell to a larger private equity firm or a corporation. In some cases, the company may be taken public.

A significant portion of leadership team compensation will be in common equity, or stock options, that sits behind the private equity firm's ownership in payout. This creates a levered effect for the value of the company. If the company performs poorly, or often just "ok," the equity of leadership is worth little, or nothing. If the company performs extraordinarily well, it can be a huge windfall for leadership. Make sure you understand, and your executive team understands, what your options will be worth under different scenarios.

A private equity fund is the ideal buyer for a company that wants to grow more aggressively and is up for big changes, even radical restructuring. For the seller, they typically pay a majority of the transaction price in cash upfront, assume complete control, and can offer a second bite of the apple if you remain in leadership and the company performs well.

What is X?

Throughout the book, you'll see references that look like algebra (e.g. 3-6X EBITDA). Any time the X is followed by a financial term, the X is creating a multiplication function (3 times EBITDA).

If the X is not followed by a specified term, which shouldn't occur often in this book, but occurs far too often in real life, it is critically important to ask: what exactly is X? Some will assume it is EBITDA. Others will assume it's cash flow, EBIT, or, in some cases, revenue. Defining "X" keeps both buyers and sellers from wasting time.

Private equity funds differ on the amount of equity they normally buy. Some "growth equity" funds will buy a large minority stake with control provisions and put the company on a defined path to another sale. Most purchase a controlling stake (51% or greater) to maximize return potential and lead operational strategy.

As a seller, you can expect private equity funds to be aggressive in their pursuit of your company. They're professionals and know that time is the enemy of all deals. Based on their specialization, they will have dedicated teams working on a strict, thorough, and well-defined due diligence process. Given the time restrictions, private equity firms will often pursue many opportunities concurrently, knowing that most will likely fall apart. If all goes well, they have the option to choose the best transactions to close, while leaving the others without a buyer. As a seller, try to know where you stand so that you do not waste time and effort with a firm for whom you are a second-string, or possibly even a fifth-string, candidate. Here are the big questions to ask:

- What is the size of the fund and range of equity check size for each investment?
- How many investments have you made in your current fund and how many more do you intend to make?
- When is the termination date for the fund?
- When was your last fundraise and when do you plan to fundraise again?
- How do you structure the capital? Are you using preferred equity, senior debt, and mezz debt? Can you map out the waterfall of proceeds in a typical exit?
- How much debt do you typically employ?
- Who makes the decision to invest? Does anyone have veto rights? Can you walk me through that process?

- Who is performing due diligence? What outside resources will be used and what are their roles versus your team's roles?
- Post-close, who leads the board of directors? What roles does the board have versus what types of decisions are delegated to the leadership team?
- Can you walk me through how big decisions are made?
- Out of your last five letters of intent, how many of them closed? What were the causes of failure?

If you find the answers not making sense, keep digging and try to get resolution before spending considerable time.

Fundless Sponsors

Fundless sponsors (or "independent" sponsors) operate similarly to private equity groups in how they acquire, hold, and manage businesses, but without dedicated capital. They source capital on a deal-by-deal basis, which adds complication to how deals are structured and makes them far less likely to close. It is estimated that only one in ten fundless sponsor deals close <u>after</u> a signed letter of intent, compared to around a quarter of deals generally.

Typically, fundless sponsors come in two flavors, with the first being former private equity staffers. After working at a private equity firm, they decided to go out on their own, bringing along relationships with LPs, knowledge of how to source and complete transactions, and (hopefully) operational experience. They recognize the headaches that come with raising and managing a fund, and have chosen to work with LPs on a deal-by-deal basis.

The second type is a retired big-company executive. Usually, they have led a division of a large organization and have made good money, but don't have enough saved for retirement, or to complete an acquisition on their own. They may be able to secure the funding, but securing "investors" in such a casual fashion usually comes with consequences like misaligned expectations and unpredictable involvement.

When a fundless sponsor finds an attractive deal on which they'd like to close, they call on their contacts, usually wealthy individuals, similar to the way companies may shop debt needs to multiple lenders. Once they have the pool of capital required and have negotiated terms, they are ready to close on the transaction. Some are looking solely to invest and take a board position, while others are also looking for a job. It's important to distinguish between the two, depending on the needs of your company.

As a seller, a fundless sponsor can be a decent alternative to compare against traditional private equity funds. For you, the transaction would likely be similar, and the sponsor will be judged by their investors on their ability to grow that specific investment, rather than the overall fund, possibly giving your company more priority. The potential challenges rest in the unknowns:

- What is the sponsor's ability to complete the transaction?
- How secure are the funding sources?
- What if your company needs more capital for growth, or to weather a storm?
- What control does the sponsor have relative to his investors? What if they disagree on strategy?
- What timeline does the sponsor have to "flip" the company?
- What experience does the sponsor have in smaller companies, how they operate, and what to expect?
- What expectations does the sponsor have for her involvement, role, and compensation?
- What if the sponsor becomes unable to lead the investment any longer?

As a word of caution, we often encounter fundless sponsors' big promises on competitive deals, but sellers tend to "circle back" to us because those sponsors possess little ability to complete a transaction. When that happens, we're happy to step in and give the company another close look.

From the outside looking in, it's hard to understand what's really going on. There are some very talented, well-connected, and reliable fundless sponsors, but most talk a bigger game than they can deliver. Here are specific questions to ask during the vetting process:

- How many deals are you currently working?
- How many of them are currently under due diligence?
- Of your last five transactions that went under a letter of intent, how many closed?
- When did you complete your last transaction?
- Can I speak with the seller about that deal?
- Who funded that deal, and will they also be funding my deal?
- How many transactions have you completed? In what industries?
- How many companies do you currently manage?
- How do you split your time between those companies?
- May I speak with 2 or 3 of your portfolio CEOs?
- Have you ever acquired, worked for, or led a company of my type?

Search Fund

A search fund is the over-caffeinated younger brother of the fundless sponsor. Just joking—well, half-joking.

A search fund is capital raised by one, or a few recent MBA graduates searching for a business to buy and operate. Historically, Stanford and Harvard are the largest originators of these acquirers, although other universities are starting to offer classes about search funds and bill them as alternative career paths to investment banking and corporate jobs.

The investors provide enough capital, usually between $250,000 and $500,000, for two years of searching. If successful in finding a candidate for acquisition, the investors who funded the search have priority to fund the transaction. Upon closing, the searcher will typically assume the CEO role, leading day-to-day operations of the company. This makes search funds an attractive option for companies that lack non-owner leadership.

Based on their post-close intentions, search funds typically only pursue control-oriented opportunities, and usually complete buyouts (100% of equity). Searchers want a company they believe will benefit from an infusion of youthful energy, technical expertise, and a commitment to growth.

Obviously, the major concern with searchers is their relative lack of experience. If the company's future is a priority for you in choosing a buyer, it's important to understand a searcher's background, experience, intentions, and ideas to determine if they are equipped to lead your company.

Here are questions to pose:

- How long have you been searching and when is your termination date? How does that impact your decision-making?
- How much control do you have over the acquisition decision? How does that process work?
- What are your search criteria? Does my company fit your search criteria? If not, why do you think your investors will make an exception?
- What type of position do you plan to assume within the company post-close?

- Do you intend to retain senior management?

Family Offices

While the previous three buyer types deploy capital on behalf of others, family offices directly invest their own money in companies. A family office is an organization built to serve a wealthy family's (or group of families) interests. This can be everything from the management of homes to building a portfolio of investments, including direct investments in companies.

Family offices are like families—no two are the same. Some have billions of dollars dispersed across multiple generations, while others have tens of millions of dollars concentrated in one person's holdings. Some are focused on particular companies in certain fields, while others operate a diversified portfolio, with public, private, real estate, and commodity holdings. Some have specific industry expertise, while others will be non-operational and have no background in business, or investing. Historically, family offices were considered passive, providing capital to managers who deployed it. However, family offices are increasingly investing directly into private companies. Many have modified their structure and team to reflect capabilities normally associated with traditional private equity groups.

As family offices have grown in number and sophistication, the ability to intimately understand and positively influence investments has been identified as the path to higher returns. By investing directly, family offices can be more flexible in what they deem to be an acceptable investment than they would be as an LP. They can also determine the holding period that makes sense for their family. For some, that may reflect a traditional 2- to 4-year holding period, while others may have an investment strategy that retains companies for decades.

The ideal company to be owned by a family office is going to depend on the family office's profile. Some will be largely passive, and the company must not expect to rely on them. Many focus on non-control, minority equity investment opportunities. Others have professional managers and plan to provide strategic and financial support to their investments. They will typically be more interested in control equity or buyout opportunities.

As with other buyer types, the critical questions revolve around getting to know the traits and characteristics of a specific family office. Example questions include:

- Are you passive or active?
- What are your core competencies?
- How do you support companies in which you invest?
- How do you view risk?
- How long do you want to hold a particular company?
- How do you typically work with leadership?
- In what other private companies are you currently invested?
- May I speak with an operator at one of those companies?

Strategics

All the buyer types outlined above are considered "financial" buyers because their primary buying motivation is to earn a financial return on the assets of the company as part of their investment portfolio. The other broad category of buyers is called "strategics." A strategic acquirer is an entity that is making an investment to strengthen their competitive position. Obviously, a strategic doesn't want to lose money in the investment process, but the reasons they buy transcend the target's current finances.

Strategics have historically paid higher prices than financial firms. In theory, this is because they know the industry intimately, have the ability to use the same assets more effectively, or can bring new assets to the table, thereby increasing the value of the acquired company. However, in recent years, financial firms have become more competitive because they consistently have capital that needs to be put to work and utilize high levels of debt, which has been cheap and available, while strategics' tolerance of higher purchase prices has grown less quickly.

Within strategics, there are two categories: competitor and extension. These categories describe why the company believes it is a "strategic" move to invest.

A strategic acquiring for competitive reasons is generally buying market share, can "synergize" duplicate costs, and often cross-sell other product lines. Almost always, they will pay more for your business, but your business will bear little resemblance post-close. At the extreme, sometimes a competitor will be bought and shut down. That may seem like an expensive way to put a competitor out of business, but the purchaser gains customer lists and proprietary assets that made the company a threat in the first place.

A strategic acquiring for extension reasons intends to add capabilities either in the form of vertical or horizontal integration. This acquired firm will usually remain intact and adapt to the new company's systems and processes.

Most companies make "build or buy" decisions when extending business lines. They can build a capability from scratch, investing time and energy into talent, research & development, testing and implementation, or buy a company that already made those investments. For many companies, acquisition is perceived as less risky, and is therefore a popular path to expansion.

One common strategic acquisition stems from dependency. If you need widgets to make your machine and you have only one supplier for those widgets, that widget maker becomes an existential risk. If that widget factory closes or is sold to a competitor, the company is in trouble. Dependency can drive up valuation, or, if the selling company is dependent, the valuation can be lowered dramatically.

Strategics come in all shapes and sizes. Sometimes, the acquiring company may be of similar size to the seller's entity. In some cases, it may be considerably smaller. On the other end of the spectrum, plenty of companies are absorbed by very large corporations. If you are considering strategic buyers, focus on fit over size. A corporation may have a dedicated M&A team, but you may find your company is, frankly, a blip on their radar and not meaningful enough to pursue. In another context, you may be a game-changer for an organization.

Warnings related to strategics revolve around expectations for post-sale activities. It is likely that not everyone currently employed will be retained due to redundancy. It is likely that your brand will eventually disappear, though this is sometimes negotiable. And, especially in large corporations, it's likely that you will have to stay on for several years and earn out some of the purchase price. For many sellers, this is the first time they will report to a boss, and it's not always a welcome change.

The ideal organization to be acquired by a strategic is going to know in advance which company should buy them and why. It will be obvious to you, if not them, that the core members of your team and collective output will add value to their existing activities. If you have a compelling case to make, you can generally command a higher valuation in such circumstances.

Role of Advisors

Advisors always play a crucial role in a transaction. While this may be obvious, it's worth stating: Great advisors are incredibly helpful, will shepherd you across the finish line, are worth a ton, and should be compensated well. Terrible advisors are incredibly damaging, will screw up an otherwise good situation, and often still get paid well.

Bar none, picking a great team of advisors is the most important transaction decision you'll make.

A common sell-side advisory team will include a law firm, an accounting firm, and perhaps an intermediary (e.g. investment banker, broker, etc.). Generally, these helpers should have the following traits.

DEEP EXPERTISE: People become excellent at something through repetition. If your lawyers help complete real estate transactions, do traffic tickets, divorces, and provide broad legal advice, chances are high they'll be awful advisors for a business sale. The same goes for accountants and intermediaries. You need to find advisors who specialize in the specifics of your situation.

ALIGNED INCENTIVES: As the proverb says, "Whose bread I eat, his song I sing." How you structure the "bread" matters. If your advisors bill you by the hour, they'll likely take their time. It's not malicious, it's human. If part of their fee is driven by an outcome, they'll likely drive towards that outcome, in both good and bad ways. No advisor's fee schedule is set in stone so be thoughtful about how you incentivize them.

PALATABLE PERSONALITY: You don't need to have your advisors over for Sunday BBQ, but you should be able to have a good working relationship. Remember, you're going to spend a considerable amount of time together under high stress. If the relationship doesn't feel right in the beginning, it's only going to get worse.

TRANSFERRED TRUST: It's crucial that you trust your advisors. There will be ten thousand ways they could cut corners, give you bad information, or generally screw you over. They're there to give you advice and help you navigate the inevitable choppy waters. If you don't feel comfortable that they'll have your best interests at heart, don't engage with them.

A great way to develop trust is by talking with their past clients. As a tip, don't only chat with the ones they recommend.

SHOCK ABSORBER: Deals are stressful. I guarantee that things will get heated, especially towards the end. A helpful advisor knows this, can anticipate the friction, and act as a shock absorber. If your advisor doesn't exude patience, that should be a big concern.

WELL-CONNECTED: In almost every deal, something unfamiliar arises. This is handled in two ways—the advisors muddle through it, or they call a friend. You'll be far better off if your advisor does the latter, but doing so requires an excellent network to draw upon. This is a big advantage of going with a bigger firm. They often have deep, niche expertise that can help you in unexpected spots.

Finding An Advisor

Great helpers are rare and thus difficult to find. I've rarely met a lawyer who doesn't claim to be able to do a transaction, or an accountant who isn't able to help. So how does one find the dream team? I'll defer to a member of the actual Dream Team, Larry Bird:

When Larry Bird was going pro he knew what he didn't know. He was a farm kid from French Lick, Indiana without any connections to the world of professional sports. He needed an agent and didn't know where to turn. He sent a letter to the top agents and asked for a response.

The request is similar to what's likely in your head. He wanted to know about their background, history, and references. But that was all for show; it was a red herring. The last question he included was, "If I don't select you as my agent, who would you recommend I choose?" He wanted to know who the people with the most information would select for themselves. Not surprisingly, everyone recommended the same person and that's who Larry selected.

I'd recommend you do the same. Ask intermediaries, accountants, and lawyers who they would choose, other than themselves. Triangulate the responses and spend your time focusing on those select few.

Should You Use An Intermediary?

At a minimum, you must hire a competent attorney and accountant to advise you during the sale process. But, there's a decision to be made around a general deal advisor, also known as a broker, intermediary, or investment banker. They're all labels for the same general thing: it's someone who spans the sale process, providing services that help you complete a transaction.

While there are broad categories, no two intermediaries are the same. Some run very strict processes akin to an open auction, while others are highly selective to whom they shop a deal. Some provide years of consulting to prepare a business for a sale, while others are only briefly involved. Some prepare all your materials, function as your deal's back office staff, negotiate your transaction, and lead due diligence. Others merely charge a fee to make the market, bringing together buyers and sellers.

Assess what you need and who can provide it. Ultimately, someone has to do the work. There's going to be a seemingly endless amount of data to produce and decisions to make, both of which depend on expertise. It's naive to think that an otherwise busy leader and their staff could somehow wedge in an extra 20 to 40 hours/week of work, often for months at a time. That's not a sales pitch for hiring an intermediary, it's reality.

To help you self-diagnose, let's break the work down into pieces by asking questions:

Where Can One Find an Intermediary?

The intermediary market is heavily fragmented. Beyond asking accountants, financial advisors, and legal advisors for recommendations, there are organizations and certifications that can be helpful to use as a filtering mechanism. Organizations and certifications to research include:

- Accredited in Business Valuation (ABV)
- Alliance of Mergers & Acquisitions Advisors (AM&AA)
- Association of Corporate Growth (ACG)
- Axial
- Certified Valuation Analyst (CVA)
- CM&AA Certification
- International Business Brokers Association (IBBA)
- M&A Source
- M&AMI Certification

Keep in mind that intermediaries come in all different types. Some may be willing to travel across the country to work with you. Some specialize in specific industries. Some only work on a referral basis. Finding the right one for your situation should require considerable investment of time and energy.

- Who will source potential buyers, vet them, sort them based on viability, field requests, and arrange for phone calls and site visits?
- Who is going to gather and organize the complete history of my firm? This includes detailed financials stretching back at least a decade, customer contracts, vendor contracts, employment agreements, legal actions (threatened or pressed), and real estate agreements.
- Who will negotiate the deal, including the business decisions for the letter of intent, the subsequent due diligence, and final paperwork? There are roughly five hundred decisions that will need to be made/negotiated during the process.
- Who is going to keep me emotionally in check during the grueling process?
- Who will be focused on the transaction and proactively

pushing the deal forward on my side of the table? What happens if that person fails?

- Who will I call when I'm not sure who to call? (Other than Ghostbusters...)

If you feel comfortable with your ability to navigate these questions, an intermediary may not be necessary. But as a word of caution, if you've never participated in, nor completed, a transaction of this nature, you're likely lacking a helpful knowledge base. As Mark Twain wrote: "A man who carries a cat by the tail learns something he can learn in no other way."

The worst path is to hire an intermediary who isn't capable of serving your needs, gums up the process, and costs a ton. You need to select an intermediary who has the firepower to get the job done, will select for the right buyer, and will gel with your resources. They should fit you and not the other way around. Here are some questions you should consider when selecting an intermediary:

- Price aside, do I care who buys my business? If not, an open auction will likely produce the highest price.
- If I do care who buys my business, what matters to me? This will determine the universe of potential buyers. The more restrictions you put on who the buyer needs to be, the fewer buyers will meet that criteria and the harder they will be to find. This may mean that you need to hire an intermediary to do your searching, or that the pool of options is so small, it's best handled personally.
- Do I already know who those buyers are? If so, then the "buyer discovery" function of an intermediary is worth less.
- Do my buyers need education about my industry in order to understand my business? If so, can I gather the

information and present it well? (Industry research data is less important to buyers.)

- Can I select a great lawyer and accountant to help with the transaction? If so, the advisor network of the intermediary is less valuable.
- Do I feel capable of producing the necessary documentation? If so, the back-office function is less valuable.
- Do I have the expertise and can I spend the time to properly vet potential acquirers? If so, the buyer vetting process is less important.
- Can I successfully negotiate the major deal terms? If so, the negotiation function is worth less.
- Can I manage my emotions and keep a level head under an unusually high amount of stress? If so, the psychology function is less valuable.

Great intermediaries have a thorough understanding of each company they represent. They've spent time building trust and understanding. They present opportunities honestly. They've prepared their client to understand the challenges of selling and tempered their expectations. Most importantly, they have committed to working to find the *right* buyer—not the easiest one or the one that earns them the quickest and biggest commission check.

Like hiring a great employee, hiring the right intermediary should take time. Evaluate multiple candidates. Ask for references. Walk through their approach and process. Discuss their experience in your industry, geographic region, company size, and preferred target buyer type. Evaluate whether you will be comfortable working through an arduous process with them. Dine together. Ultimately, go with the group you believe has the best incentives and will get you to the best outcome.

Like any service provider, there are excellent ones and terrible ones. Here are a few brief cautions:

- If they only pay you compliments, you should keep looking. Your business isn't flawless, and if they can't see the flaws and be honest with you about them, they won't be able to effectively market your business.
- You don't want to be the whale, minnow, or guinea pig. If your business is large, it's almost always best to go with a bigger firm. If your business is small, don't seek out the Wall Street investment banker you know from college. And while some inexperienced intermediaries can be fantastic, I would be skeptical of being anyone's first transaction.
- If the intermediary's fee structure does not depend heavily or exclusively on selling the company, I would question what you are paying for.
- If the intermediary advocates for hiding or manipulating information, even if it's "just until we get under LOI," run. Run fast.

There are good intermediaries out there and adventur.es has had the pleasure of doing deals with some of them. But, like many industries, gold is mixed with dirt and rocks. You have to sift through the chaff to get to the wheat.

Hopefully the decision to hire an intermediary is obvious. If it's not, I'd suggest hiring one. The sale process is much harder than you expect, even taking into account that you expect it to be hard.

Financial Structures

When most people hear that a company has been sold, their first question is, "How much?" They're asking about valuation. Unfortunately, the valuation of a company is anything but straightforward. What matters is how much money traded, under what conditions and terms, for what level of ownership of the business, and behind what debt.

One of my favorite things to do is explore announcements of high-profile startup fundings. I'm always curious about what lies beyond the headlines. People hear that a company recently achieved "unicorn status," reaching the rare $1 billion valuation. What you don't hear much about are liquidation preferences, or how much money must be returned to the latest investor before anyone else gets a dollar out. You rarely hear about preferred returns, or a compounding dividend that automatically dilutes other owners. When those details are taken into account, the valuation seems far less rosy.

As you'll see, no two valuations are the same, even if the headline number is identical. A $10 million all-cash, all equity offer with no contingencies and no clawbacks is a heck of a lot more valuable than a $10 million offer with $5 million of senior debt, $2 million of subordinated debt, $1 million of seller debt, $1.5 million of earn-out, and $500,000 of equity. My point: details matter. On a financial basis, what matters is the amount, timing, and probability of cash.

Valuation

"There are numerous profitable smaller firms in traditional industries with established business models and moderate growth prospects that routinely sell for EBITDA multiples of 4X to 5X."

—The Market for Smaller Firms (Harvard)

The "transaction value" of a company is the total value of the business, including assets necessary to sustain ongoing operations.

Typically, transactions exclude existing long-term debt and cash, as the buyer wants a clean slate to organize the capital structure. Apart from cash, working capital is included. Ultimately, the norm doesn't matter. It's whatever you negotiate. But it's important to fully understand the consequences of an offer.

The valuation can be based on a variety of financial models. You may have heard of some of the following: "a multiple of EBITDA," "a multiple of EBIT," "a multiple of seller discretionary earnings (SDE)," or "discounted cash flow." All of these models, however complex they appear, seek to use the historical and forecasted earning power of the business to determine the present value of future cash flows.

The present value of future cash flow sounds like a technical term, but, broken down, it's quite simple. If you are selling me the ability to make $1 million next year, and, at least in theory, every year thereafter, what is that worth to me today? Investors discount those cash flows to the present, because a dollar of profit is far less valuable in ten years than it is this year.

The Waterfall

The waterfall represents how money is distributed during a transaction. In understanding the waterfall, keep two things in mind: 1. Most transactions do not deliver all cash at close, and 2. All parties are not necessarily, or even by default, equal.

In general, debt "eats" before equity, senior debt eats before subordinated debt, and preferred equity eats before common equity.

As an example, a company is sold for $100M that carries $50M in senior debt and $20M in subordinated debt. There's preferred equity, which sits above common equity, of $10M that has a 2X liquidation preference. How much would a 20% owner of common equity receive of the sale proceeds? Perhaps surprisingly, only $2M.

There are many reasons why structural tools that change the waterfall exist. It limits certain parties' risks, and depending on the circumstances, can help protect the solvency of the company. However, as a seller, it is important to understand how each tool is implemented, and how it affects your proceeds.

As you may have noticed, each model uses a multiple of something. As any business owner knows, that "something" can fluctuate without affecting the value of the business — one-time expenses can make a business look less profitable and one-time revenues do the opposite. The trick is to determine what counts and why.

There is no set multiple for a specific business, but you can get an approximation based on the transactions of other companies of similar size, industry, and business element (i.e. leadership, financial consistency). Here's a table of common multiple ranges of SDE and EBITDA by company size.

Company's Earnings	Common Multiple Range	Enterprise Value Range
Under $500,000 SDE	1.5-2.75X SDE	Under $1.375M
$500K to $1M SDE	2.5-3.5X SDE	$1.25M to $3.5M
$1M to $2M SDE	2.75-3.75X SDE	$2.75M to $7.5M
$2M to $5M EBITDA	3.5-6.5X EBITDA	$7M to $32.5M
$5 to $10M EBITDA	4.5-8X EBITDA	$22.5M to $80M

Note: SDE includes the owner's compensation, while EBITDA excludes owner compensation. The owner's typical involvement determines the difference in valuation methodology. Smaller companies usually have involved owners and the buyer will often be the operator, resulting in the use of SDE for valuation.

Resources used to build this table include: Pepperdine University's Private Capital Markets Project, Pitchbook, Pratt's Stats, The Business Reference Guide, and studies by Harvard University and Stanford University.

To illustrate how multiples work in the marketplace, here are a few examples of the calculation:

- A company earned $2 million in EBITDA last year. The two years prior it earned $1 million per year. One buyer may offer 4 times $2 million, resulting in an enterprise value of $8 million, while another buyer may average the 3-year performance, offering $5.3 million (4 times $1.333 million).

- A company earned $5 million in EBITDA last year, but the year before it earned $8 million. A buyer interpreting that company to be in substantial decline may offer $17.5 million (3.5 times $5 million), or possibly lower. Another buyer may have a strategic opportunity to boost that business back to its previous performance level, and may offer $20 to $25 million.

- A company in a highly cyclical industry earned $4 million last year. A buyer may request a full cycle of historical financials and average the cycle to determine the earnings on which it will base its valuation.

- Three years ago, a company had less than $1 million in SDE. For the past two years, business has exploded, resulting in EBITDA of $3 million and $5 million. A buyer who believes the high growth is likely to continue may be willing to pay 7 times trailing twelve month EBITDA.

Once the valuation is determined, the deal comes down to what portion of the business is being sold and under what terms. It is common for less than 100% of the equity to be sold, and for the seller to have a portion of the price paid out of future earnings, called an earnout, and/or a loan given to the buyer by the seller, called a seller note.

Seller notes and earnouts kill a handful of birds with one stone. At the base level, it's a way for sellers to have skin in the game, aligning interests. These structures provide leverage on the equity, increasing the anticipated return and the multiple the buyer can pay. Seller notes and earnouts also share risk. When it comes to company operations and prospects, sellers are always in a superior position of knowledge

Math, Explained?

Your company's recent performance:

2 Year's Ago EBIT: $2 million

2 Year's Ago EBITDA: $2.5 million

Last Year's EBIT: $3.75 million

Last Year's EBITDA: $4.4 million

TTM EBIT: $3.6 million

TTM EBITDA: $4.25 million

Projected EBITDA: $5 million

Here are possible enterprise value calculations:

5X Two-Year Blend of EBIT: $14.375 million

4X Last Year's EBITDA: $17.6 million

4.5X TTM EBIT: $16.2 million

3.5X TTM EBITDA: $14.875 million

4.75X Projected EBITDA: $23.75 million

You can see how quickly your business can generate a wide range of valuations. However, beware, it's just a headline number. The devil is in the details, and each one of these offers is likely to include a different structure of payments and protections. Keep reading to learn more about those.

to buyers. These structures provide a way for the seller to "put their money where their mouth is."

Terms and Deal Components

There's an old saying, "You set the price and I'll set the terms." That's because, in many ways, the deal components are more important than the purchase price. The terms outline risk allocation, the cost for delaying payment, and how future efforts of all parties will be compensated.

Adjustments and Deductions

Because deals often take 6 to 18 months to come together, the purchase price is usually dependent on a multiple of moving variable. For instance, a 4X multiple on adjusted trailing-twelve-month (TTM) EBITDA means that the buyer will pay based on how the company continues to perform, with certain adjustments. This can be favorable if the company continues to perform nicely, or stressful if things take a turn for the worse. Another option is to fix the timeframe from which the calculation will be made.

Both parties will pay close attention to any adjustments made to the earnings calculation. Sellers will want to increase earnings by adding back exorbitant owner salaries and benefits, personal expenses, one-time and non-recurring costs, above-market rent if the real estate is owned by a related party, and payroll for family members not working in the business. Buyers will want to reduce earnings by deducting capital expenditures, under-funded working capital, market compensation for owner duties, a reserve for warranty issues, and an estimated amount of non-recurring costs that always seem to pop up.

The goal is to get an accurate representation of the business's true earning power. While this may seem straightforward, agreeing to what is added and subtracted can be contentious. For instance, how much is the owner worth to the business? Most owners will say, "not much," and try to reduce the associated compensation to a minimal amount for their expertise. Buyers will often argue the opposite—an operator with 20+ years of experience and a solid track record is worth a lot.

Cash At Close

	Offer 1	Offer 2	Offer 3	Offer 4
Enterprise Value	$20 million			
Cash at Close	$10M	$10M	$10M	$10M
Equity	$5M	$4M	$10M	$2M
Senior Debt	$5M	$4M		$4M
Subordinated Debt		$2M		$4M
Seller Note	$10M	$10M	$10M	$10M

The first component of the financial deal terms is the amount of cash at closing. This will be a combination of equity, senior debt, and subordinated debt. Equity is the amount of cash the buyer is injecting into the deal. Senior debt is usually a bank loan, which holds the most senior position on the assets. If there is a default, the senior note holder gets paid back 100% before anyone else.

Next in line is subordinate debt, which is often called mezzanine debt ("mezz debt"). Usually mezz debt comes with quite onerous terms to compensate the lender for an under-secured, or subordinated, position. If the company can't pay back the senior lender in full, the mezz debt holder gets nothing, and because it's not guaranteed, the lender can't use other assets to get repaid. Common terms for mezz debt include a high interest rate, often between 12-25%, and an equity "kicker," between 2-7% of the company's equity, that sweetens the deal. Interest terms and other covenants may track with the company's performance, increasing or decreasing depending on EBITDA, or other metrics.

It's common for equity to be a fairly small percentage of the overall closing cash, perhaps as low as 15%. This can leave a considerable burden on the company in debt payments. Senior debt likes to get paid back quickly, often in five years or less, while mezz debt can be more flexible. Mezz debt is frequently paid-in-kind, which means that while the senior debt is paid down, the mezz debt accrues interest without a cash payment. This can be attractive for cash flow, but allows the more expensive debt to compound into a higher burden in the future.

Capital Structure Table
Senior Debt (e.g. Bank)
Subordinated Debt (e.g. Mezz)
Seller Debt
Preferred Equity
Common Equity

Seller debt is often subordinate to all other debt of the company. In the case of a highly leveraged company with a poor outlook, this can make seller debt payments extremely unlikely to be repaid. In contrast, the risk of default may be low-to-moderate if the company is lightly leveraged and stable. It just comes down to the situation. It's crucial to understand how the debt is stacked.

Behind the debt, but above common equity, can be preferred equity, which means an ownership stake that carries with it characteristics different from other equity. Often preferred equity will have a debt-like payment attached to it, or a preference in how proceeds upon a liquidation get distributed. It's important to understand under what scenarios the preferred equity gets a preference and what it will mean for common equity holders.

Regardless of the source and terms, a buyer's use of debt or preferred equity will create a discount to the common equity value, including any equity rolled forward by the seller. If you sell 70% of your company and most of the cash at closing came from debt, the 30% you retain will be worth considerably less than the same 30% before the transaction. Said differently, since the company is now paying off debt and interest, and you are a 30% owner, you're now paying for 30% of the debt that you did not have before. Therefore your equity, which is in line behind the senior debt, mezz debt, seller debt, and preferred equity, is worth less.

Earnouts

Earnouts are payments tied to the future performance of the business. A buyer finds these especially useful when the operating history of the company is choppy, or there are questions about how the company will perform. On the seller's side, some earnouts can include favorable terms that allow their total proceeds from the sale to grow significantly. The goal of an earnout is to align the owner's interests with those of the buyer and mitigate some of the operating risk. In situations where the buyer and seller disagree on future earnings projections, earnouts help bridge the gap by allowing both sides to take a wait-and-see approach to a portion of the valuation.

Earnouts can be tied to virtually any metric, or event, including pre-tax earnings, EBITDA, gross profit, revenue, add-on acquisitions, employee retention, customer retention, owner's employment duration, cost reductions, or the achievement of other milestones. If it can be measured, it can be structured in an earnout.

With that said, earnouts also carry a fair amount of trepidation, and rightfully so. Operating a business is challenging, relationships can become strained, and an unscrupulous buyer might decide to alter the business so that the metric being used might appear different from the business reality. The further the metric is down the income statement, the more likely this is possible. For example, it's easier to play with pre-tax net income than gross profit, and much easier than revenue.

It's crucial that you do your homework on a buyer.

- Do they have a history of contentious post-close relationships?
- How durable is the acquirer, and will they be around in 5 to 10 years?
- If the worst became reality, how easy is it to move the goalposts? What recourse would you have if they did so?

Net Working Capital Calculation

Current Assets
(Accounts Receivable + Inventory + Prepaid Expenses + Cash)
− Current Liabilities
(Accounts Payable + Other Current Liabilities)
_____
Net Working Capital

By definition, net working capital is current assets minus current liabilities. Working capital is usually calculated as accounts receivable, inventory, and prepaid expenses, minus accounts payable, short-term debt like a line of credit, and accrued expenses. Sometimes cash is negotiated to be left in.

While this sounds straightforward, one of the most challenging parts of any transaction is calculating net working capital. Each of the working capital line items is, to some degree, discretionary. What is the proper amount of inventory? Well, it depends on your business model and the situation. Sometimes you can buy in bulk and save some margin. Should that dramatic increase in inventory be counted against the seller? It depends. The seller added the inventory to increase earnings, which is compensated for in the multiple they're being paid.

What if the company uses "just-in-time" inventory? That efficiency cuts both ways. In one sense, the buyer should happily take fewer assets because they are acquiring excellent systems and the extra assets aren't needed. But those fewer assets reduce the liquidation value of the company and the just-in-time nature of the business can be inherently risky. So what is the proper inventory level? That's a matter of negotiation.

Some buyers will outline the net working capital amount required as a specific number in the offered terms, while others will indicate a calculation to be used and a future date for calculating the final amount.

Fees

Depending on the buyer, another component of the deal might be fees. Historically, private equity firms have charged the company for any intervention they provide. These take the form of closing fees, monitoring fees, financing fees, travel fees, transaction fees, termination fees, consultancy fees, and/or sales fees. Some are fixed, some

On-The-Books Vs. Bookable Inventory

If you've ever had a bank evaluate your inventory for lending purposes, you likely experienced the difference between what exists versus what counts. Most buyers will do the same. If you have outdated or damaged inventory listed on your balance sheet, it is unlikely that the buyer will accept it as part of transferrable net working capital. They only want to take possession of inventory that is "bookable" as sales.

are flexible. It's common for most professional investors to take a fee for monitoring the investment in the form of a flat fee of $100,000 to $500,000 per year (highly dependent on company size) or between 1% and 5% of EBITDA. That fee may, or may not, include travel expenses. As a tip, if excluded from a flat fee, setting a travel budget can be helpful to avoid awkward conversations around the price of jet fuel.

Other fees are less common, but not uncommon. Some private equity funds take a fee at closing for their work in the transaction. They might also do so if the company is sold. If the private equity firm decides to refinance the company and dividend out cash, they might take a fee for handling the new debt.

Private equity firms have been known to put their executives into consulting roles, or take a finder's fee for helping the company secure new business. Some agreements include "acceleration clauses" or "termination fees" that require the company to pay all the future fees that could be owed to the private equity firm if the company is sold.

Understand what fees will be charged, how they are calculated, and under what conditions.

Employee Compensation

While each situation is unique, it's not unusual for the buyer to put an additional employee compensation program in place. In traditional private equity this might be called an "employee option pool," which will get distributed upon achieving a high level of performance over a period of time. The tricky part is the fine print. These programs look attractive on the surface, but require high performance, which often doesn't manifest. The bar is intentionally high.

This is important for a seller because it can create another dilutive event, usually upon a subsequent sale. If the company accomplishes enough to where the option pool kicks in, things are usually in a good spot. But not always. Unless the options are both dollar-weighted and time-weighted, meaning that both the return on invested capital (ROIC) and internal rate of return (IRR) matter, they can produce perverse consequences for owners.

Risk Allocation: Reps and Warranties, Caps and Baskets, Covenants

The seller is always in a superior position of knowledge and will be asked to assert things are true about the company at closing. A claim is called a representation, or a "rep." In some cases, the seller will agree to be held financially responsible for something being true, called a warranty. This can be as simple as, "I warrant that I own the company and have the power to transact." Or it can take the form of guaranteeing that the financials are as presented. These promises are bundled together in the purchase agreement under a section often called "Indemnification."

A covenant is a promise that something is either done, will be done, or will not be done. Common covenants include getting leases transferred, agreeing to post-close financial arrangements, or maintaining a certain level of financial strength. It's anything the seller is agreeing to abide by.

With reps and warranties, the seller is accepting risk and the nature and extent of that risk is governed by caps and baskets. Caps are the limits to the amount of risk, as measured in dollars, that the buyer can recoup from the seller if damages arise. The basket is the minimum dollar threshold of damages that must be met for any indemnification. Remember, there will always be small, unforeseen costs. Based on the type of reps and warranties, the caps and baskets can differ. While this sounds complicated, it's straightforward when explained by an example:

To make things simple, let's say the purchase price is $10 million all cash at close. The cap is $5 million and the basket is $100,000. This means that no matter what happens, the maximum amount that can be recouped from the seller is $5 million of the purchase price. But in order to start being indemnified, the damages must reach $100,000 in total. Think of it like a deductible on your insurance. This ensures that the buyer isn't "nickel and diming" the seller, while also not letting the buyer defray all the risk. A "tipping basket" allows the buyer to recoup all damages once the threshold is met, including the amount of the basket.

The source of repayment depends on the deal. A portion of the purchase price can be held in escrow. Future payments can be offset, also called an offset right. The seller may personally guarantee the indemnification. Or, there might be a corporate guarantee provided.

Some investors, particularly larger private equity funds, may employ something called Reps & Warranties Insurance. Instead of structuring an escrow or some other backstop to warranty information is true, they take out insurance.

Real Estate

Many business owners purchase real estate outside the company as a way of extending their returns. When it comes time to sell the company, the real estate inevitably becomes part of the equation. Some buyers are happy to buy the real estate along with the business, but most are not. Operating companies and real estate are very different assets, with wildly different risk and return expectations. Most buyers will want to negotiate a lease.

It's important to include those returns, if they're above market rate, in your company's valuation. If the real estate is strategic, the buyer will also likely want an option to purchase the real estate. The trick is to understand how the real estate interplays with the operating company, and how to use it as a bargaining chip.

The dynamics are fairly obvious: the seller will want a long-term triple-net lease with a favorable cap rate. The buyer will want a low-cost, short-term lease with many options to renew at a pre-agreed upon escalation of rent. If the real estate is flexible, meaning it has many uses, the seller has more room to negotiate. But if the real estate is single-use, it can be important for all parties that the company use it indefinitely.

A good place to start is a fair market value (FMV) appraisal. The buyer will always be skeptical of the appraisal, but it's a jumping-off point for negotiation. Next, it's important to understand common cap rates, or the rate of return expected for real estate investments net of taxes, fees, and labor. Cap rates start around 5% for large, long-term leases from extremely creditworthy tenants and go up as high as 15% for short-term, risky, high-maintenance tenants.

For small businesses, the real estate cap rate should normally fall between 7% and 11%. It's common to have 3- to 5-year leases, with multiple options to renew, and a 2% to 4% yearly escalation in rent.

Employment/Consulting

The last piece of the puzzle is post-close compensation. It's common for the seller to receive a salary, or a consulting fee, for their work in the business. The importance of your post-close compensation largely depends on the nature of the transaction. If you're planning to exit stage left quickly, compensation can be irrelevant. But if you're planning to continue working in the business, your compensation plan can be crucial.

Using A CAP Rate

HYPOTHETICAL SITUATION: You purchased property used by your company. As part of your agreement with the buyer, they have an option to buy the property for a 9% cap rate.

If they exercise this option in the future, here is how the value is determined if the lease is "triple net (NNN)," or the rent is independent of the taxes, maintenance, and insurance, as well as utilities:

Current Year Annual NNN Rent: $360,000

Occupancy: 100% by Your Company

To calculate the total value to be paid, divide the annual net operating income by the cap rate (360,000/.09).

Real Estate Value to Be Paid in Sale: $4 million

There's a chasm between leadership and consulting, so you should discuss expectations with the buyer. If the buyer intends to keep you on in a leadership role, your compensation should reflect the value you add to the business, including customary bonuses or other forms of incentive compensation. Consistency is key. If you agree your value to the business is $200,000, then it logically follows you'd get paid $200,000 for your continued role. But before you demand a raise for yourself, remember that compensation increases will be deducted from the earnings, and thus the valuation. Since the business value is usually a multiple of earnings, you should carefully weigh the financial trade-offs of a salary verses an incremental sale payout.

If you maintain a consultative role, your compensation for that time may be structured as an agreed upon hourly rate or an annual salary. Your agreement will almost always include a non-compete/non-solicit clause that restricts your ability to start a new competing firm, join a competing firm, or hire away employees. You have decades of relationships and goodwill built up. The buyer wants to ensure that you won't use those as a weapon, and will transfer those as part of the transaction.

The Negotiation

The first section of the book focused on your reasons for selling. Before beginning negotiations, revisit your goals.

First Move

By the nature of how transactions come about, typically the buyer makes the first move. They will provide a rough valuation range and terms for consideration. In almost all cases, unless explicitly stated otherwise, the buyer expects you to counter.

The initial move may catch you off guard, positively or negatively based on your expectations. It's important, though, to remember the end game and try to stay objective. And there are a lot of details. In the initial offering stage, the primary goal is to determine whether it's likely that you and the prospective buyer are in the same ballpark. If so, you'll continue to work through details until the days before closing.

Some prospective buyers will give you an opportunity to tell them what your transaction priorities are. You can always be forthcoming about your priorities in both marketing documents and on management calls. In my experience, transparency around expectations and goals aids in expediting negotiation and helps both parties avoid wasting time on a poor fit.

Valuation vs. Terms

As a seller, it can be easy to fixate on the numbers. "My business is worth X. I'm going to get Y cash at close." These figures will represent some of the largest you've seen in your lifetime. The focus on valuation is understandable, but remember that structure and terms are equally important in negotiation.

When negotiating with a qualified and trustworthy investor (a.k.a. the type of buyer you probably want), you should take advantage of their expertise. While this may seem counterintuitive, they have spent their careers understanding creative ways to structure a deal, from responsible options and uses of debt to how to properly incentivize existing leadership to ensure a smooth transition. Your best path is to tell them what is important to you and why, and also what you recognize to be the risks in the deal. Then let them explain what options may satisfy both parties best. To be clear, I'm not suggesting blind trust in a buyer regardless of reputation, or your intuition. Always approach a proposed solution with open-minded skepticism.

To illustrate, here are a handful of scenarios:

QUICK EXIT: You tell the buyer that you will only consider an offer that provides all cash at close because of grave health concerns. Immediate liquidity is priority number one. You are asking the buyer to assume all responsibility and liability for not only the future prospects of the organization, but also the transition post-close. The buyer will apply a discount and the resulting valuation will likely be substantially less than a deal with more structure over a longer time period.

MARKET-BASED EXIT: You tell the buyer that you have a target valuation range, providing research that backs up why you believe it is reasonable for your business. The buyer will compare your research against their own, and also the circumstances of your company. Sellers sometimes bring forth research on industry-relevant companies unrelated in scale, leadership depth, and earnings history, which a buyer will quickly disregard. If the research is valid, however, the buyer will likely calculate a similar valuation range (it may not be exactly the same, but they'll tell you why) and focus on structure and terms. What percentage will be earned out to ensure performance? What guarantees will be outlined about key employees and customers?

BRIGHT FUTURE EXIT: You tell the buyer the company is set up for future growth, you have confidence in the projections provided, and, while you need some immediate liquidity, you want to share in the upside. The buyer will structure the deal to share risk and reward.

Valuation and terms will be varied, and that's a good thing. They're creative solutions. It's key to remember what's important to you and evaluate the options against those criteria. And above all, communicate your interests clearly.

There are no hard rules in valuation. A buyer doesn't have to match another buyer's offer, accept your presented adjustments, or meet your demands on timeline or payment structure in their offer. And, you don't have to sell. Every value and formula is negotiable.

Formula vs. Numerical Values

Prospective buyers each have their own way of valuing companies. You may encounter offers structured as a calculation of a future number rather than a specific current value. For instance, one private equity firm may value your company at 4X trailing twelve months (TTM) earnings before interest and taxes (EBIT), while another group may say your transaction value is $8 million and expect that value to hold during the due diligence period.

As you may suspect, each technique carries its own advantages and disadvantages for both sides. With finite numbers, you have a better understanding of how the transaction will play out, but it leaves the most recent positive performance out of the equation.

If the offer is based on a multiple formula, there are far more unknowns. It might help the seller if current performance is strong, or add another point of negotiation and deal complication that could derail closing.

As an example, the valuation may be based off of TTM earnings, with the calculation set to occur three weeks prior to closing. As the seller, you may plug in the values to determine the likely numerical range, only to discover three weeks prior to closing that the majority of the adjustments you made to earnings for non-business expenses are considered unacceptable by the buyer. Upon calculating the final figure, you may be millions of dollars apart, just based on differences over what counts as an adjustment.

Another major area of risk when using a formulaic approach is in anticipating the closing date. If your company experiences fluctuation in performance, you may find yourself looking at less than favorable final figures on things like net working capital. As discussed in other parts of the book, just because you make it to due diligence, doesn't mean the transaction will close, and it is even more unlikely to close on the targeted date.

As a point of reference, investors who use a formulaic approach generally take between 12 and 36 months of performance into account to determine each value. This means your enterprise value may be based on a multiple of a 36-month EBIT blend, while your net working capital requirement may be based on TTM.

Walk in the Buyer's Shoes

Investors don't buy things to lose money. They expect a financial return. So, while you should be paid for what you've created, if you cannot make an argument for how the buyer will earn a decent return, your valuation is unlikely to hold up to scrutiny. Roughly, smaller private equity funds, search funds, fundless sponsors, and wealthy individuals will likely expect between a 20-35% return, depending on strategy and opportunity costs.

Sellers often tend to focus on growth projections when marketing their business and beginning negotiations. For a buyer, future growth is *unproven*, especially when the growth rate is expected to positively deviate from historic performance. Said another way, high growth can be fantastic, or terrible, or non-existent depending on circumstances. As such, buyers put little weight on projections. That said, as multiples go up, there is a greater expectation for substantive growth plans.

A superior marketing strategy is to highlight proof of health. What those proof points are depends on the type of business. For some, you may be able to highlight consistency in gross margins, net margins, client relationships, pricing power, and/or market position. Pointing out market indicators of relative health can also be helpful; if, for instance, you can prove you are the largest firm by volume or revenue in your industry or geographic region, that is of value to the investor's consideration set. Third party verification of data points related to competitive positioning will always carry more weight.

When walking in the buyer's shoes, think through how to make them comfortable, which also means acknowledging known risks. If, for example, your industry is cyclical, explain the maximum fluctuations you've previously experienced, over what time period, and how the business is positioned to avoid historical low points in the future. Also explain how the company weathered the challenges. All businesses fluctuate. It's not something to hide.

BATNA

When considering offers, always have a BATNA, an acronym for the "best alternative to a negotiated agreement." In the simplest terms, BATNA represents your perceived safety net. It's your alternative. If negotiations fail, you have your BATNA. You never want to accept a deal that is less favorable than your BATNA.

Depending on your circumstances, your BATNA may be another buyer, an employee stock ownership plan (ESOP), or continued ownership of the company. Some buyers are fine with playing second fiddle, letting you see if you can get more, but knowing that, at worst, you can come back to their offer.

In most situations, offers will not allow for an easy apples-to-apples comparison, so be sure to understand the details involved in both sides of any comparison, as well as concepts like the time-value of money involved in each structure.

I am not ashamed to say that we have been recognized as a BATNA by some owners in the past. They wanted to see if they could get something better and asked us to wait. Sometimes we will, other times we won't.

General Negotiation Tips

Every prospective seller and buyer will have a different negotiation style. Most styles work just fine, as long as you stick to one. Every negotiation has the same building blocks. Start by asking the right questions:

- *"What are the most important and least important components of the deal to you?"* This serves to identify win-win opportunities, where each party's different interests are served differently. Be sure to pay attention to the order in which they discuss their interests. They'll likely be close to a forced-ranked list.
- *"What parts are deal-breakers?"* This helps you understand the rigidity of the other group. If you're having trouble understanding why something is a deal-breaker, be sure to follow up with additional clarifying questions.

- *"If you assume the deal falls apart, why did it happen?"* Make sure they talk about things on both sides that could go wrong. If there's something like debt financing that could clearly be a challenge, specifically bring it up.
- *"What are the types of things you could discover during due diligence that would cause the deal to fail?"* These are going to be their hot-button concerns and areas you should be prepared to deep-dive on during due diligence.
- *"Who else is a decision-maker on the deal other than you and the immediate team?"* You'll always want to know if you're negotiating with the decision-maker, or a representative of the decision-maker. It's not always obvious.
- *"How are the negotiation team, due diligence team, and post-close operational team different? Who leads each part of the process?"* Often there are different actors involved as the process proceeds. It's important to understand those dynamics.
- *"How much of the negotiation will be done principal-to-principal and how much will be conducted through our lawyers and accountants?"* This points to the formality of their process and will give you a better idea of the legal/accounting bills you'll face.

Once you have a good handle on the other party's viewpoint, interests, and concerns, you should focus on what matters to you, what matters to them, and where you can trade things. Think of the negotiation process as a chess board with a series of swaps. If they're going to take your knight, you want two of their pawns. It's important that your options and board pieces are clearly defined, and that you know what you're willing to give up under what circumstances. Usually the party least willing to budge on price is more willing to negotiate on terms.

Paperwork

Once the parties get past the bulk of exploratory due diligence, attention turns to the documents needed to consummate the transaction.

Drafting and Timing

Drafting documents is expensive and time-consuming, with most transactions falling between $50,000 and $500,000 in legal fees and taking a couple weeks to arrive at a first draft. It is customary for a buyer to create the documents, which typically include a purchase agreement, operating agreement, employment agreements, seller note, seller-owned real estate lease, and bank documents if there's a lender involved. Because of the expense and time commitment, the drafting party will want to delay drafting until completing the bulk of exploratory due diligence. In fact, a great signal for the progression of the deal is the involvement of legal counsel and the delivery of first drafts. A buyer delaying legal engagement is a buyer still deciding whether to move forward on the deal.

Nitpicking and Grandstanding

Lawyers are people too and come with the same kaleidoscope of opinions, emotions, and biases as the rest of us. The importance of picking a good lawyer cannot be overstated. Good lawyers understand the nuance, fight for what is important, and do it with grace and tact. Bad lawyers grandstand and nitpick, driving up the cost of the transaction. In short, hire someone who is reasonable and experienced in lower-middle market transactions.

Purchase Agreement

Purchase agreements come in two flavors, asset purchase or stock purchase, but functionally contain many of the same terms. The biggest difference is how risk is divvied up. A buyer of assets can pick and choose which assets and liabilities to assume, while a stock purchaser is buying everything, including legacy risks, by default.

The first part of the agreement will include the material deal terms like information about the types of payment, when the payments will be due, and what can be done with those payments in the event of a problem. It should include every meaningful understanding between the parties.

It's important for the buyer to understand exactly what is being bought, and for the seller to understand exactly what is being sold. The purchase agreement will contain a list of material assets. If something isn't listed in an asset purchase agreement, it's not being sold. But if something isn't listed in a stock purchase agreement, it still might be included, but it's not guaranteed.

As an example, working capital is a key component of every deal, and is generally defined as inventory, accounts receivable, prepaid expenses, and potentially cash, minus accrued expenses and accounts payable. Straightforward, right? Buyers will want only undamaged and saleable inventory counted, which begs the question about what is obsolete. There's no universal definition, so it becomes another point of negotiation.

As an example, consider the following balance sheet:

Current Assets		Current Liabilities	
Cash	$800,000	Accounts Payable	$250,000
Accounts Receivable	$950,000	Other Current Liabilities	$300,000
Inventory	$2,200,000		
Prepaid Expenses	$50,000		
Total Current Assets	**$4,000,000**	**Total Current Liabilities**	**$550,000**

The simplest calculation would be Current Assets less Current Liabilities ($4 million — $550,000), equaling $3.45 million in net working capital. But is cash included? Should the balance sheet be normalized because the business is seasonal? Is the business undercapitalized for growth, or overcapitalized to satisfy a third party's mandates (e.g. bonding requirements)? There can be many complications.

Other major components are the representations and warranties, or what promises the seller is making to the buyer about their knowledge and the degree to which they guarantee their knowledge is correct. This part is all about what risks exist, what happens if risks are undisclosed, and who assumes responsibility for the risks, known or unknown. While this may seem mundane, it's an incredibly important part and often where the biggest conflicts occur.

To illustrate, consider lawsuits and disputes. The seller will usually disclose them to the buyer in the form of a schedule. But who is responsible for the litigation of them, or resulting consequences? What if a dispute pops up related to activity before the business transacted? What if the seller knew of a problem, but no lawsuit had yet been filed? These are the grey areas that will be governed by the representations and warranties section.

The last big piece of the purchase agreement will be taxation, with both parties agreeing to what parts of the transaction will be taxed which way. The government will get its due, so the question is how the responsibility is divided. The seller wants as much of the purchase price to be taxed at the capital gains rate (lower taxes), while the buyer has incentives for the seller to pay ordinary income taxes on the proceeds because it allows the buyer to depreciate the assets and gain a tax benefit.

Operating Agreement

If you're selling 100% of the firm, the operating agreement is irrelevant. Don't worry about it and move on. If you're going to be a partner after the transaction, it's important to understand your rights, decision-making authority, and/or ability to block a decision. The operating agreement lays the groundwork for company governance and owner relationships post-close.

Operating agreements allow for virtually any agreement between parties to be memorialized, including preferred returns, unusual decision-making authority, or the need for consent. This is useful when deals become complicated with earnouts, seller financing, or owner-operators that remain in leadership post-close.

Seller Note

Often, deals are partially financed by the seller in the form of a note. Besides the obvious note term and rate, it's important to understand what would cause a default, as well as your remedy.

Seller notes are often subordinate to, or "sit" below in priority, all other company debt. If the company doesn't perform well enough to pay off the senior debt, the seller note often remains unpaid. In that event, it's important to understand your guarantee. If it's personally guaranteed, then it means people, usually the buyer(s), backstops the note's payments. Corporate guarantees are using other companies, including their assets and income, to secure the note. But most often, the company itself will be the guarantor. This means that you can take back the assets and stock of the company in the event of a default.

Each of these types of guarantee may be extremely valuable, or worthless, depending on the strength of the guarantor. If someone has no assets and very little income, does it matter if they sign a personal guarantee? But if your guarantor is a Fortune 500 company, the likelihood of nonpayment approaches zero.

This makes examining the assets backing up any guarantee essential. If everything goes as planned, this never becomes an issue. But just as the investor works to understand their downside risks, you should understand yours. Here are questions you should ask:

- Have you, or your firm, ever defaulted on a note? If so, can you explain the circumstances?
- Can you show me your financial statements, or produce a bank letter attesting to your financial strength?
- Can you help me understand under what circumstances my note wouldn't be paid?

Employment/Consulting Agreement

Most smaller companies rely heavily on their owner(s), which makes post-close employment agreements common for sellers. Like any agreement, you should understand the basics: responsibilities, wages, bonuses, and benefits. But sometimes seller employment agreements are an important part of the sale process. In that case, the term of employment becomes a key point.

Most employment agreements are at-will by default, meaning that the employer can fire the employee for no cause. An exception is when the employment agreement is compensation for the value of the business. In that case, it's important to negotiate a term of employment, typically 2 to 5 years, and include a buyout clause that provides a lump-sum severance in case of termination. Virtually all seller employment agreements will come with non-compete/non-solicit clauses.

Lease

For sellers with real estate, leases can be a fantastic source of future income. If you're selling a business, you're likely familiar with leases and the components. It's important that you think of leasing as just another piece of your financial returns, which always includes a risk profile. A long-term, above-market lease can serve a similar function as a consulting agreement, but without it being tied to performance.

Fees & Costs

Great advisors are rare and highly valuable, hence they get paid well. You will need a lead transaction attorney and a lead outside accountant. If you're used to spending a minimal amount on low-stakes legal issues, transaction fees can be a shocker. Don't look at them as a zero-sum. Often a great advisor will charge you a lot <u>and</u> save you money.

All told, expect roughly 3 to 15 percent of the transaction proceeds to be spent in the process, with a minimum spend of $25,000. That's a wide range and necessarily so based on the levels of complexity, size of transaction, industry dynamics, and buyer choice. Generally, the larger the transaction, the higher the numerical cost, but the lower the fees as a percentage of the transaction.

Legal
Fee rates will depend on whether you choose an individual lawyer or a firm, and their respective areas of expertise. Generally, sell-side legal work is done on an hourly basis and hourly rates vary based on seniority, specialty, and geographic location. Flat fee and adjustable rate structures exist, but usually only to investors as they will have a history on other deals and know the relative scope of what they seek.

Choosing the right lawyer should involve reviewing more than just their fees and rates, but typical hourly rates range from $225 to $1,000. On a $10 million transaction, you should generally expect to spend between $40,000 and $100,000 in legal costs. To make you feel better, the acquirer will be spending twice as much.

If you have a particularly complex deal (e.g. multiple entities and sellers, intricate post-close structure), fees will trend higher. If you use a high-cost, but deal-inexperienced attorney, fees will be higher. If the transaction gets restructured multiples times during due diligence, or advisors start warring over "who's right," or some nasty issue pops up, fees will be higher. However, if there's high trust between the seller and buyer, the transaction is very straightforward, and no senior lender gets involved, transaction fees can be dramatically lower.

As in other industries, there are groups trying to disrupt the traditional legal engagement framework, so you may find something unusual in your search. However, I would caution you to seek level-headed experience above all else. This is one of the times where "innovation" isn't particularly helpful.

Accounting

In most cases, you will work with existing financial advisors on a stepped-up basis, unless there's something particularly unusual or intricate. They'll need to prepare financial documents for marketing the company, then be able to back them up during due diligence. You'll want your accountant to interface directly with the buyer's accounting team on issues like working capital, tax matters, and add-backs.

As such, make sure to talk to your advisors early on about expected scope, associated costs, and timelines. Having an engaged and responsive accountant can be helpful in smoothing the process. Typical sell-side hourly accounting fees will be between $125 and $600 per hour, depending on the size of firm and location.

The buyer will bear most of the brunt of accounting fees, which typically include a Quality of Earnings report (QofE) that verifies the financial state of the company, pro forma financials, working capital calculations, and fraud detection. All-in accounting fees are likely to fall between $25,000 and $100,000 for a $10 million deal.

Intermediaries

To work on your behalf (known as a "sell-side engagement"), an intermediary can be engaged under a retainer fee, a success fee, or a combination of the two methods.

Retainer fees, also known as work fees, typically start at $50,000 and go up depending on the size of potential transaction. Some retainer models involve a monthly installment ($3,000 to $15,000), while others are arranged for a term at a flat fee.

Success fees usually represent a percentage of a completed transaction. The details matter in success fee arrangements, as some will require you to pay the full value of all consideration in the transaction to them at close (including cash, debt, equity rolled over, seller note, earnout). Make sure you understand what proceeds are included and when payment is due.

The success fee percentages can be structured in several ways. On smaller deals, the success fee may be a flat percentage—usually 6 to 12%—of the transaction. On large deals (over $50 million), that flat percentage can drop to as low as 1.5%. The workload required by an intermediary to close a deal does not differ tremendously based on the size of the transaction, and actually can be less work for larger companies considering the increased access to resources.

The most common success fee structure we see used in both sell-side and buy-side engagements is the Lehman structure. Under Lehman, you pay:

> 5% on the first $1 million
> 4% on the next $1 million
> 3% on the next $1 million
> 2% on the next $1 million
> 1% on the remaining total

"Modified Lehman" terms involve altering the percentages (i.e. 6/5/4/3/2, or 1.5% on the remaining total). Although we rarely see it, "Double Lehman" doubles the percentages (10/8/6/4/2).

Some intermediaries employ the opposite of Lehman, called a reverse scaled success fee, in which the percentage rises based on the total amount. This obviously incentivizes the intermediary to seek out the highest possible price above all else. As with lawyers, working with an independent intermediary usually means lower costs than working with a firm. But buyer beware. An upfront "discount" may not pay off in the end.

If you engage an intermediary, you will be expected to pay at least a portion of their fee at closing. If an intermediary engages you under the guise that the buyer will ultimately cover your fee, I recommend choosing another intermediary. At best, you will frustrate the buyer and cause trust issues. At worst, the investor will walk when the "game" becomes apparent.

Investors also sometimes engage intermediaries (known as a "buy-side engagement"). The fee structures are similar and their marching orders are to go find potential sellers that are not actively trying to sell their business. There's a good chance you've been contacted by one before. Buy-side intermediaries should not be charging you anything to introduce the potential buyer, as their fees are already covered. To do so is playing both sides, and is unethical.

The Process

Once you've decided to look for a buyer, you enter the acquisitions process.

Preparing to Market

If you've ever had a hand in your company's marketing strategy to customers, you know that there are many ways to market a product or service. The same is true for finding a buyer. Every process starts with the basics.

Your goal is to take all the complexity that makes up the current business, team, and future opportunity and turn it into something easily consumable by potential investors. As previous sections outlined, be clear about your objectives and priorities so that you don't waste time on inappropriate potential matches.

Below are descriptions of information to gather and resulting documents to prepare:

Financial Statements

You will want a summary version of the income statement for marketing purposes. The summary should include each year's revenue, cost of goods sold (COGS), gross profit, gross margin (gross profit as a percentage of revenue), net income, net margin (net income as a percentage of revenue), depreciation/amortization, and earnings before interest, taxes, depreciation and amortization (EBITDA).

EXAMPLE SUMMARY	2016	2017	2018
Revenue	$10,000,000	$15,000,000	$20,000,000
COGS	$5,000,000	$6,000,000	$9,000,000
Gross Profit	$5,000,000	$9,000,000	$11,000,000
Gross Margin	50%	60%	55%
Pre-Tax Net Income	$2,000,000	$5,000,000	$6,000,000
Net Margin	20%	33.33%	30%
Depreciation/ Amortization	$100,000	$150,000	$250,000
EBITDA	$2,100,000	$5,150,000	$6,250,000

You will also need to prepare at least three years of income statements and balance sheets. If your business is cyclical, prepare financials for the last full cycle. If your business is seasonal and/or has major net working capital fluctuations, prepare monthly statements for at least the past 24 months. Expect to share the detailed income statements after the potential buyer signs a nondisclosure agreement.

The complications in preparing financial statements arise when making adjustments for personal and extraordinary one-time expenses. You can try to adjust anything out, but expect buyers to ask questions and make their own assessment of earnings. To briefly illustrate: If your personal country club membership is on the books, it's clearly not a cost the new owner would assume and is therefore a valid adjustment. If you try to adjust out the cost of developing your website, something obviously required in business operations, you will find no buyers accept it. If you try to adjust out employee bonuses because they're "discretionary," you can expect buyers to ask: do your employees look at those bonuses as discretionary?

The two question sets to evaluate when making adjustments to financials are:

- ON SEEMINGLY PERSONAL EXPENSES: Is this an expense related to me personally that will not be assumed by a new owner because it bears no professional value? If yes, there is an argument to be made for the adjustment. Common adjustments of this type include personal cars, travel unrelated to work, family employees who will not continue post-close, and family cell phone plans that are being run through the business.
- ON EXTRAORDINARY/DISCRETIONARY ONE-TIME EXPENSES: Is this expense unlikely to be repeated? If it would not have been paid in the first place, would the company's operation or culture have suffered?

  The most common type of adjustment is an add-back for charitable contributions made by the company. Outside of that, some sellers and intermediaries will attempt to make arguments for adjustments of lawsuits, travel expenses, high salaries, and/or bonuses. Very few of these add-backs are accepted, and may erode trust as the buyer perceives the earning power of the business has been manipulated, or they are being set up poorly.

Many intermediaries prepare projection summaries forecasting the future performance of the business. As a buyer, I can tell you we don't rely on these and don't spend much time looking at them, except as a gauge of expectations. Forecasts often take a slow-growth company and say it will double, or triple, its growth rate upon sale with nothing more than a change in ownership.

Depending on the relevance and expense to obtain, cash flow statements may also be worthwhile to prepare. They will help the buyer understand the fluctuations, capital expenditure needs, and the variability of working capital.

Teaser/Blind Profile

The teaser is your elevator pitch, comprised of general information about yourself and company shared prior to a buyer signing a non-disclosure agreement. If you are reaching out directly, hiding the company's name is nearly impossible. With an intermediary, the teaser can present a description of the company, and references to the regional location(s).

The critical information to disclose in a teaser includes:

- What your company does
- Where you are headquartered (at least the region of the country)
- Company type (i.e. S-Corporation, LLC, etc.)
- 3-year summary financials, including any adjustments
- TTM financials, including any adjustments
- References to company's scale (i.e. number of employees, amount of products produced)
- References to company's main competitive advantages
- What type of transaction you are seeking (i.e. buyout, majority recapitalization, growth investment)
- Contact information for how to inquire about further details, if interested

A teaser should be only one page in length. For discretion, it is acceptable to use ranges on non-financial information (e.g. 30 to 50 employees).

Non-disclosure Agreement/Confidentiality Agreement (NDA/CA)

If a buyer becomes interested in your company after reviewing the teaser or being introduced by someone who knows you are seeking an investor, to protect yourself and the company, you will execute a simple non-disclosure agreement (NDA). An example is available at www.adventur.es/mutual-nda/.

If you are using an intermediary, review their NDA. Some intermediaries attempt to use their agreements to protect personal motives (i.e. getting paid by seller, buyer, or both) rather than those of the company they represent. My firm does not sign NDAs that include clauses making us liable for things in which we have no involvement (e.g. a seller's agreement and structure for compensating a sell-side intermediary). If your intermediary plays games like that, understand that it will negatively select for the buyers they're able to bring to the table.

An NDA should protect the information you share with interested parties from being used for competitive purposes or shared with parties who have not obtained your permission. That's it. And it gives you the peace of mind to be able to share information candidly.

Confidential Information Memorandum (CIM)

When a buyer becomes interested in your company and has signed an NDA, they want to dive into the details to determine whether the opportunity is viable. One way to do this is through hours of communication, whether by phone or written Q&A. An alternative is to prepare a confidential information memorandum (CIM), which covers the information you expect all buyers to find of interest.

Depending on the type of business, a CIM may include:

- An overview of the company's operating history: founding date, any past transfer of ownership, how it grew from its origins to where it is today

- Organizational details: locations/facilities, employee count, products/services offered, legal structure
- Leadership details: who are the key people, for what are they responsible, to whom do they report, and how is the owner involved
- Customer details: number of accounts, how they are acquired and managed, any concentration issues, retention metrics, and what constitutes a profitable target customer
- Competitive position: points of differentiation, most important competitors and why they are competitive, threats from related industries
- Detailed financials: full cycle of income statements and balance sheets (as referenced earlier)
- Growth plan: may be quantitative (detailed financial projections) and/or qualitative (expansion opportunities)
- Material skeletons: if there is something negative about the business (i.e. pending lawsuit) that may make it unattractive, disclose it
- Transaction and Transition details: tell the potential buyer what you want them to know before making an offer

Some CIMs are 8 pages, others are 65, and some are PowerPoint presentations with embedded video explanations. The length or look is not the goal. Communicate what the next owner needs to know. The only time style counts is when it's painfully obvious that very little work went into the presentation. Don't do that.

Other Operating Documents

Depending on the specifics of your business, it may be useful to prepare other documents as appendices to the CIM. Examples include:

- Organizational chart of employees
- Sample exclusivity agreements with suppliers or distributors
- Compensation and tenure of employees
- Details surrounding a particularly large customer (i.e. contracts)
- Current backlog of work
- Asset list

There is no required timing or pace to sell a business. If you prepare the documents, but don't feel ready to talk to buyers, just wait. Buyers want to talk to sellers who are seriously considering selling. It could be 6 months or 2 years from the date of the first conversation, but if you do not feel ready to engage with buyers, don't do it. You want to avoid burning bridges, and nothing turns off a buyer like a seller who plays games.

Buyers are a different breed from your employees, customers, or suppliers. They are going to ask you about your failures and shortcomings, and those of your team. They are going to ask you about the good years and the bad ones. For many owners, it can be a somewhat unsettling dialogue. But, at some point, it needs to be shared.

Creating a Market

Once prepared, it's time to create a market of potential buyers. Assuming you've read the section on Types of Buyers, I'm going to focus here on quantity and quality of buyers, and how to contact different types.

	Auction	Hyper-Target	Likely
Distribute Teasers	50-3,000	1-3	30-40
Distribute CIMs	50-1,000	1-2	20-30
Management Calls	Usually wait until after IOIs	1-2	8-15
Site Visits	Usually wait until after IOIs	1-2	4-10
IOIs	8-25	1-2	3-9
LOIs	1-5	1	1-3
Due Diligence	1	1	1

Auction

One approach to creating the market is mass distribution. Inform anyone you believe may have interest in buying your company, or may know someone who does.

Online platforms have increasingly enabled businesses to be sold in this fashion. They are publicly listed, giving anyone the ability to inquire.

It may create a bidding war, giving the owner many viewpoints on how the business is valued and the ability to choose the best offer. However, an offering meant for "everyone" attracts no one particularly well.

Many buyers will self-select out of an auction-oriented process because it's not worth their time. As a base rate, if there are 100 potential buyers, then each individual buyer has a 1% chance of being the "winner," and probably less than a quarter of a percent chance of closing on the deal. It's hard, as a buyer, to get excited about such small odds, regardless of the business.

If you do choose an auction process, there is a certain amount of "corralling" that has to be done. This usually includes putting deadlines to certain steps in the process for all interested parties, forcing decisions based on a desire to keep things moving, rather than on the belief that the right buyer has necessarily been found.

If money is your only motivation in selling, an auction can be a viable path to selling. However, as I've touched on in several parts of this book, eye-popping offers often don't close, so it's important not to lose sight of reality in the drama of the process.

Hyper-target

On the other end of the spectrum from an auction-oriented approach is to hyper-target. You pick the one buyer you want to buy the company, and make your highly personalized pitch on why them, why now, and under what terms.

There can be a lot of noise in the mergers and acquisitions world that looks like progress. A hyper-targeted approach cuts out the noise entirely. You have the direct conversation, determine if they're interested, and, if so, negotiate the details.

Common hyper-targeted scenarios include reaching out to a corporation in the same industry for which your business would represent a line extension or vertical integration. It can also be an investor you particularly admire or, if you are seeking an owner-operator, the right person for the job.

Hyper-targeting can be far more efficient in obtaining the desired outcome of selling, but comes with risks. A lack of competition will usually create a lower selling price. With only one buyer, you might also get within a foot of the finish line and lose the deal, only to start over again.

The Likely Market

In most selling situations, the best path forward is somewhere in between. Determine who should be invited to participate by quickly removing buyer types you don't want, and then prioritizing what characteristics are desirable. Once you have the attributes of a buyer prioritized, it's time to research. Buyers have come a long way in marketing themselves, so you should be able to find basic information online.

Start with a simple Google search. Test different keyword combinations. Use LinkedIn to search by industry and geography. Explore deal-specific resources like Association for Corporate Growth (ACG), Private Equity Info, and Axial. Ask your trusted advisors for recommendations.

Once you have a target list assembled, it's time to prioritize again. If there are two or three clear favorites, start by contacting them. If you are not satisfied with the outcome of those initial discussions, or they do not have interest, keep moving down the list. Ask those that pass if they know of other groups that may be a better fit, continuing the research in-process.

Connecting with Targeted Buyers

Although you may feel anxiety when contacting a potential buyer for the first time, understand they talk with sellers often. Don't overthink it.

Typically, potential buyers will have someone who is the appropriate point of contact for a new opportunity. In strategically-targeted corporate buyers, depending on their scale, this may be the CEO, COO, or someone who works in corporate planning, or mergers & acquisitions. Among financial buyers, the appropriate contact is usually listed on their website. If the group only has two or three team members, you can contact anyone. In larger groups, there will be a "Deals" or "Opportunities" team. If you're seeking a search fund, it may be worthwhile to contact MBA programs with search fund programs and ask for recommendations. If you cannot find a specific person to contact, you can always submit an email requesting contact information for the appropriate person.

Typically, initial outreach to financial buyers is by email. It can be this simple:

> *I am interested in exploring options for* [describe the type of transaction you are seeking]. *I came across your firm and think it may be a good fit because...* [describe why you're contacting them].
>
> *I have attached a PDF that provides a brief overview of our company. Please let me know if it may be of interest to you.* [Attach the teaser.]
>
> [Insert contact information]

Depending on the competitive dynamics with a strategic buyer, you may want to get an NDA signed before disclosing much. Executives with experience in mergers & acquisitions will understand when you say, "I have something I'd like to discuss with you about our two companies, but first I'd like to get a nondisclosure agreement in place."

Like sellers, buyers come in all shapes and sizes. Some are great at communication, while others find it challenging. You may hear back from one group in ten minutes, while others may take several weeks to respond. While you should take that into account as a touchpoint, feel free to follow up. But if they don't respond within a week, I'd recommend trying a different point of contact or moving on. Serious buyers don't waste opportunities.

If you are using an intermediary, they will likely do the initial outreach on your behalf, using a blind teaser. Remind them of your objectives in creating the best market for your company, so that you do not find yourself with a large quantity of buyers that lack the attributes you are seeking.

Rejection

Buyers reject businesses all the time. For most, it's the norm to pass on an opportunity after only reviewing the teaser. As discussed in Types of Buyers, good investors often recognize quickly when something is not the right fit. When a group passes, it is not necessarily a judgment on the quality of your company.

Some groups will pass for cause. They may say, "Your client concentration is too high," or point out some other flaw. While being judged is never fun, try to take it for what it is: constructive feedback from the market.

To this point, you always have the opportunity to reject a potential buyer. If someone doesn't seem right to you for any reason, or no specific reason, you can always eliminate them from the process, or, if you are looking to keep options open, put them on the sideline for a while.

Conversations

After mutual interest has been determined, the potential buyer will sign an NDA, review your materials, and be ready to start talking. In an intermediated deal, this is known as the "management calls" phase.

Your initial call with a potential buyer will feel a lot like a first date, with both parties discussing the details of their organizations, business philosophy, and the potential buyer's approach. This first conversation tends to last between 30 minutes and an hour. At the end, it should be obvious if there is chemistry.

If it still feels like there may be a good fit, discussions will continue on. There may be written requests for specific information, another management call, or documents exchanged on both sides. The goal of all this communication is understanding. The buyer is trying to make sure they properly understand the details of the situation and the people involved. You are trying to make sure you can get along with the buyer, and that they have the required resources, the proper disposition, and the necessary skill set.

Ballpark Valuation

As long as rapport is building through each exchange and once the buyer feels they have enough information, they will provide a ballpark valuation range for the business.

At my firm, we do this before a site visit. Some do so afterwards. There is no required sequence, but we believe that you shouldn't spend considerable time with us unless we meet your broad financial expectations.

The ballpark valuation will likely be a range and can vary by millions. It depends on the size of the business and the number of unknowns. These valuations serve as market readings, and, as a seller, are much more valuable to you than any "professional valuation" you can purchase. After all, something is only worth what someone else is willing to pay for it.

Site Visit

Generally, a buyer waits to be invited by the seller to visit the company. Depending on your comfort level, you may invite them after the first management call, or wait for several conversations. Most buyers will not make a detailed offer on a company without seeing operations in person and meeting you. The more casually an offer is made, the less seriously you should take it.

A site visit is a 4- to-8-hour visit by one or more individuals from a buyer's team. The buyer will fly in and, depending on the awareness of a potential transaction among employees, visit the company under a low profile. It's important that you set expectations with the buyer about what they're supposed to say if asked for background by an employee.

While on site, the potential buyer will want to get an understanding of the culture, systems, facility, and leadership. If there are important layers of leadership beyond you, they will likely request an opportunity to meet them while visiting, however briefly.

After the on-site tour, most groups move off site to a restaurant, country club, or other meeting space for further discussions. It is likely that the buyer will want to spend several hours discussing a wide range of topics, including life outside the office.

The final component of a site visit, at least for our firm, is dining together. We relish the opportunity to get to know people personally and eating together goes a long way in that department. For the buyer, the site visit is as much about getting to know you as it is about confirming their understanding of the business.

Indication of Interest (IOI)/Term Sheet

When the buyer is ready to make a detailed offer, they will do so in the form of an indication of interest (IOI) and/or term sheet. These documents outline both how the buyer is valuing the company and under what deal structure, terms, and timeline they would transact.

While most buyers take it seriously, as a seller, it's important to remember that IOIs are non-binding. Nothing about the offer is guaranteed. Some buyers throw out dozens of IOIs each month as means of gauging market expectations and sifting through opportunities. Others use them to present a suspiciously attractive "headline" number, then slowly lower the valuation after you agree to exclusivity with them.

An IOI typically takes the form of a letter or explanatory document, while a term sheet looks like a table or spreadsheet. There's no magic to it. If it clearly communicates "the deal," it's getting the job done.

When evaluating IOIs/term sheets, it's important to note what isn't included. If the offer is overly rosy, with few details, you should question the buyer's intentions. Sometimes fishing expeditions are great ways to gather proprietary information. Or, the buyer may be extremely inexperienced and incapable of fulfilling the offer.

Buyer Qualification

When terms are agreeable to both sides, the buyer will say, "Let's draft the letter of intent and move into due diligence."

As the seller, you will want to pause at this time and verify several things. Every step of the process up to this point does not involve a commitment, meaning you are free to talk to any potential buyer and hear how they would value the business. The letter of intent almost always includes an exclusivity clause, so when you sign it, you are agreeing to cease all conversations about selling with any other potential buyer. So, confirm whether this is the buyer of choice.

The second thing to verify before signing is whether the buyer has the financial capacity to consummate the proposed transaction. This is more easily verified with groups who have internal funds (i.e. private equity groups, family offices, corporations), but if their structure includes debt, you will want to understand their banking relationships. If they are a fundless sponsor or search fund, ask for written proof of investor interest in providing the capital for the deal under the agreed upon terms. With an individual investor or owner/operator, especially if they are seeking SBA financing, you will want a statement from their financial institution certifying their financial capacity. For some, this will be a burdensome request, but feel free to remind them that due diligence is expensive for both parties and should only be invested in if it's clear that the transaction can close.

The third thing to confirm is the state of your relationships with other potential buyers. For those with whom you've been having meaningful conversations, you may consider giving them an opportunity to catch up to the buyer who submitted an IOI before beginning to work on an LOI. Or, you may simply say that you believe you've found a good match and need to move forward with them, but that if something should change in that process, you'd like to leave the door open. Most buyers will understand that they either need to get aggressive, or step aside. However, if you go under letter of intent without informing those under the impression that you were still moving at a slower pace, you will likely burn the bridge. As a courtesy, let interested buyers know within the week.

Letter of Intent

After negotiation is considered complete, the buyer will have a letter of intent drafted for both parties to sign.

A letter of intent (LOI) is a promise to agree to transact on the terms specified if the facts check out. It specifies a period of exclusivity, typically between 60 and 120 days, and obligates the seller to provide the information requested.

The other specific sections will include:

- Price
- Type of sale (stock vs. asset)
- Where money is coming from and how it will be used (sources and uses)
- Most material terms of the sale
- What needs to be resolved before a transaction can take place
- Due diligence timeline and general steps

Due Diligence

Due diligence is just a fancy term for:

- What have you told me that isn't true?
- What haven't you told me that I need to know?
- What don't you know that I should know?

Answering each question takes varying levels of understanding, information, and skill. No two transactions are alike.

Since there's a comprehensive due diligence checklist in the back of the book that covers many situations, I won't spend too much time talking about the work that must be done. Instead, I want to discuss expectations around pace, timeline, difficulty, and emotions.

There's a joke in private equity that each deal is won and lost at least three times during due diligence. Broadly, it's never an enjoyable or relaxed process, and for very good reason. Due diligence is a natural expression of skepticism and verification. The seller will always be in a superior position of knowledge and the buyer must assume they're not getting the full picture from a deal book, a few calls, and a short in-person visit.

Like going on a first date, then dating, then being engaged, and ultimately married, a company's hidden quirks, dark secrets, and weaknesses eventually come out. It's on the buyer to make sure they understand them. It's also on the seller not to surprise the buyer.

Like running a company, due diligence is a skill and some buyers are more skilled than others.

Sources & Uses

Here is an example of a Sources and Uses table for a $21M transaction:

Sources	
Senior Debt	$7M
Mezz Debt	$0
Seller Note	$5M
Buyer Equity	$7M
Rollover Equity	$2M

Uses	
Cash to Sellers	$13M
Seller Note	$5M
Rollover Equity	$2M
Company Cash Infusion	$1M

Inexperienced buyers, especially ones with aggressive lawyers, will want to send every part of the company through the equivalent of a proctology exam. That's painful, messy, and time consuming. The more skilled buyer will understand what questions to ask and what threads to tug.

Ask about a buyer's history and their expectations for due diligence. The response will demonstrate their approach, organizational skills, roles, and likelihood of close. You should ask:

- Of the last ten letters of intent you signed, how many resulted in a closed transaction?
- Of those that failed in due diligence, what were the causes?
- On average, how long do most of your due diligence periods last?
- May I talk with one intermediary and one owner that have gone through due diligence with you?
- What roles do your accounting firm and law firm play in the process?
- How is work divided amongst you and your team?
- What would have to happen for you to pull the plug on the acquisition?
- How would you describe your pace of due diligence?
- What's your average turnaround time on reviewing documents?
- How often are you planning to be on site and what type of work do you typically do when on site?
- What will be asked of my team and who specifically would you like included in due diligence?

In the lower end of the lower middle market, or companies under $15 million of EBITDA, the ratio of companies that close after letter of intent is reported to be less than one quarter. Said differently, on average there's greater than a 75% chance that the transaction won't close once it goes under a letter of intent. That may be shocking, but let me unpack the underlying causes.

To start, most smaller companies have poor information systems. There may be lots of data, but it's usually inaccurate and unorganized. This presents obvious challenges for a buyer trying to get an accurate picture of reality. On top of that, most companies are run with a minimal level of accounting staff and expertise, because most owners trust their gut more than the numbers. The attitude is usually that a ballpark is good enough, which makes sense if you have a deep expertise in your field and have run the company for a considerable period of time. The buyer needs to see what you know in words and numbers.

A buyer's level of comfort with ambiguity and skill in gathering, organizing, and processing information becomes more and more crucial the smaller the acquisition target. Intermediaries can help, but sometimes lack the necessary skill set. At the end of the day, someone has to do the work. This creates friction and can delay, or derail, the process.

Staff access is often an issue. Sometimes sellers don't want to tell their team members about the sale until it happens. This is highly problematic when it comes to leaders in accounting, finance, and human resources. The buyer needs a ton of information, which is usually challenging for the owner-seller to collect and organize. When questions arise, the buyer will want precise answers and background information to support a conclusion. While it's not impossible to get a deal done without anyone other than the owner involved in due diligence, it complicates an already challenging process.

Emotions also play a role in due diligence. Without exception, the seller will think the buyer is asking stupid, insulting, or out-of-bounds questions. Buyers, and especially inexperienced ones, will think the seller is withholding information, too sensitive, and slow to respond. It comes with the territory. On both sides, there will be "aww, screw it" moments. It's important to keep your head, be rational, and be slow to anger. Easier said than done.

As a word of caution, some buyers intentionally use this period to re-trade the deal. They will say things are not important to discuss prior to due diligence, and then, with details in hand, say that things are not as they expected and changes to terms will be required. Sometimes legitimate details are uncovered and a change to the terms is reasonable. But for some firms, it's an unfortunate strategy for showing a big, beautiful number to get the LOI signed, with no intention of closing on anything close to the proposed figure. This is why understanding the track record of your prospective buyer is so important.

The exploratory and skeptical part of due diligence can take anywhere between 4 weeks if a small miracle occurs, to over a year on a highly complex transaction with two "deliberate" (slow) parties. As part of the letter of intent, there is usually a 60- to 120-day exclusivity period, which is meant to curtail the amount of probing without an intent to close. That period should not be looked at as a shot clock, or a deadline, unless the buyer is clearly stalling. It can serve as a forcing function, but is almost always extended if everyone is working in good faith to complete the transaction.

Once the buyer becomes comfortable with the information presented and discovered, there is usually a flip to a "closing mentality." All the parties then work to get legal documents drafted, negotiated, and signed. While this sounds like a straightforward process, it's usually another big hurdle to get over, with hundreds of small decisions to be negotiated.

If you make it over all these hurdles, congrats. You've sold your company.

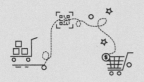

A NEW NORMAL:
Post-Close Expectations

You've accomplished an extremely challenging task and it marks the end of a life chapter. You'll likely feel good about it for a few days, indulge in a couple of celebratory dinners with the family, catch up on some sleep, and then reality will hit you like a ton of bricks. Life is different. There are new participants, shifting priorities, and ongoing challenges.

CONTENTS:
— Telling Your People,
   And Then Telling The Town
— Conflict Resolution
— Seller's Remorse

When someone sells a business, it never fails that those around them interpret the action as immediate entry into permanent vacation. In fact, the opposite is often true.

Depending on the terms of your deal and involvement, you may find yourself working more hours post-close rather than less. There will be integration initiatives, lots of communication, and potentially new people to train. Typically, even if you're bought out completely, you will stay on in some capacity for 1 to 3 years, slowly withdrawing.

If you have retained equity and intend to maintain a day-to-day role long-term, obviously your new normal now involves a partner. Self-motivated people can be jarred by having another person, or people, with influence on their priorities and schedule. It's important to talk about potential points of friction with your new partners.

Telling Your People, Then Telling The Town.

The sale of a company is, unfortunately, a great gossip topic. For friends and family, there are questions about money and lifestyle. For employees, there are questions about operations and careers. For suppliers and distributors, there are questions about consistency, quality control and relationship management. For customers, there are questions about everything.

In most cases, all that is necessary is calm, crisp communication. Confusion, or the perception of confusion, will cause far more heartburn than the actual situation warrants.

So much of communication is determined by tone. Depending on your personality, there may be a feeling of, "I've finally made it. Now I can tell everyone how successful I am." Even if that's true in some sense, I strongly encourage you not to go down that path. Change is incredibly stressful for people, especially those not in a position of control. Consider their feelings and concerns, and channel your communication to help support them and the future of the company.

Every company culture differs, so you'll need to determine, in collaboration with the buyer, the appropriate prioritization of stakeholders and what should be said. We have found that face-to-face meetings for the most important stakeholders are more fruitful for all involved, as they provide non-verbal information. As a general rule, talk to people face-to-face when you can.

Even those who should not be affected by the sale will likely have questions and concerns. Make sure to give them a venue to be heard, understood, and appreciated. In the long run, it will mean less gossip, less confusion, and a more efficient transition.

Conflict Resolution

You now have a new partner and/or boss. That's going to be odd in the same way merging two families would initially have awkwardness. Even if you made it through due diligence on relatively good terms, conflicts will arise once the ink is dry.

In due diligence, the buyer is simply confirming details and not making changes. After closing, the new partner will have ideas about how things should work. You will not like everything they propose, or agree with every change. If you did, they'd be you. Likewise, the buyer will not love some of your decisions. They may, in fact, fundamentally disagree.

It is exceedingly rare that two groups will have the exact same insight and come to the same plan of action in every circumstance, and that is true of the new operating team. For your personal health, the health of your leadership team, and the health of your relationship with the buyer, it is critically important to proactively assess how each side will work to avoid and resolve conflicts that will inevitably arise.

Proactive actions include, but are not limited to:

- Agreeing explicitly on what subjects the buyer wants to be consulted and the thresholds for involvement. A $500 decision is light-years away from a $100,000 decision.
- Agreeing explicitly on what subjects the seller should remain involved in post-close.
- Establishing clear points of contact to prevent redundancy, or people feeling out of the loop.
- Establishing preferred methods of communication. Some people talk and listen, while others prefer to type and read.
- Over-communicating for the first few months not only to assure everyone is on the same page about changes, but also to build rapport.
- Always being prepared to explain the logic behind a particular decision dispassionately and without taking the question personally.
- Maintaining self-awareness on priorities, including the highest and best uses of your time.

We're not here to write a conflict resolution guide. Hopefully you picked a reasonable and good-natured buyer. If you did, you'll still disagree and debate from time to time, but you'll both ultimately want the same thing: a healthy business and a good team.

In my experience, things start to get overly dramatic when one side either isn't communicating or is poorly communicating with the other. You've got to be willing to talk it through.

Seller's Remorse

Even if you love the buyer, are in a great place financially, and believe the future of the company is secure, at some point in the months or years post-close, you will likely wish you had not sold. It may be when you feel left out of a meeting in which you would have liked to participate. It may be when you open up your inbox after a few days to find only a handful of new emails. It may be when you hear employees reference "old ways" of doing things in the office in a condescending fashion. Or it may be when you find out that there is a material change in process with which you do not agree. Seller's remorse is a real thing and it <u>will</u> happen to you.

Every coach has a different playbook. Every captain charts their own course. This is the point at which you'll need to remember why you sold, the benefits of selling (financial and otherwise), and why you chose the buyer that you did.

One helpful idea is to maintain a notebook during the process, charting goals and decisions, and how you came to them. This way, when experiencing post-close frustration or remorse, you can go back and walk through your earlier reasoning. Hopefully, you will find overwhelming evidence that outweighs any recently discovered oversight or current irritation.

We affectionately call the most unhealthy type of seller's remorse, "damned if you do, damned if you don't." Some sellers expect perfection from the new buyer, or worse. If the buyer makes a decision they don't agree with and the outcome is negative, it's easy for the seller to become hyper-critical of the buyer. Remember, they're not screwing up your company. They're just doing something different and it didn't work out as well as expected. Remember when that happened to you over the years?

The flip side is when the buyer makes changes that dramatically and positively impact the business, creating feelings of jealousy and remorse. You should want your buyer to be wildly successful with your company and take it to new heights. If you think you'll struggle with seeing them succeed, please don't sell your company.

If you're in a reduced role post-close, you may need to go find something constructive to do with your time. I've met a lot of sellers. Some of them want to go play more golf. Some of them want to go play with grandkids. Some want to pursue a passion. But for some, work was their version of play, and they'd rather have died in their office chair. For those people, it may be useful to start looking around for opportunities.

APPENDIX A
Jargon Glossary & Shorthand Abbreviation Reference

Amortize: v. Spreading a repayment, cost, or deduction over a period of time

A loan equally amortized means it will be paid in equal installments each year. Intangible assets amortized means the asset's value will decrease each year for tax purposes.

Annuity: n. An investment that provides annual cash flow to its owner

There is a financial product called an annuity that provides a fixed amount of income per year, but in a broader context, it means the investment regularly distributes cash.

Assign: v. The legal act of transferring property and/or ownership rights from one party to another

When you sell something, you are selling it to a specific party (a.k.a. the entity that sends the cash). When you buy something, you want to make sure everyone knows you own it. The legal process for this is the assignment.

Balloon/Bullet Payment: n. The amount due after a designated amount of time

Most notes are paid in installments, while others have a lump sum paid at the end of the loan. These are known as balloon, or bullet payments.

Binding: adj. Legally agreed to
The purchase agreement is binding.

Call/Put Options: n. Options are an obligation for the purchase or sale of an asset. A call option refers to the buyer's right to "call" the other party's asset. A put option refers to the seller's right to "put" the shares.
As a seller who is rolling forward equity, your put option provides a contractual right to liquidate your remaining interest. Conversely, the buyer's call option is their contractual right to force you to liquidate your remaining interest.

Cap Rate: n. The rate of return on real estate, based on the income generated
A cap rate can be used to negotiate the sale price of a building. If a building has an annual net operating income of $180,000 and both parties agree it should be sold at a 9% cap rate, the price will be $2,000,000.

Cap Table: n. A table of who owns the equity, what they paid for it, and their financial rights
If you're not listed on the cap table, you are not an owner.

Caps & Baskets: n. A "cap" is the total amount of damages the buyer may recover from the seller. A "basket" is the minimum monetary threshold that must be met before a buyer can demand reimbursement for damages.
A seller will want a large basket and a small cap. A buyer will want a small basket and a large cap. Risk tolerance and negotiation determine where they meet in the middle.

Capital: n. Money
"How much capital do you have?" is the equivalent of asking how much money a party has available to be used for the deal.

Cash at Close: n. The amount of cash delivered by the buyer to the seller at closing
If a buyer offers all cash at close, you're either selling a sure thing, or the price is low.

Closing: n. The event at which cash is exchanged and assignment is made between buyer and seller
The process isn't over until Closing.

Collateral: n. Something of value pledged as security for repayment of a loan or other payment obligation
Collateral is what's collected in the event of default.

Committed Capital: n. A pool of capital in the bank, or contractually committed by Limited Partners, used to fund a transaction
An offer backed by committed capital is much more likely to close.

Confidential Information Memorandum (CIM)/Offering Memorandum (OM): n. A document or presentation that outlines the company's history and material deal points to prospective investors
Most investors will say no after reviewing the CIM. What you're left with are those who want to dig into the details.

Consideration: n. Form(s) of payment
Cash, equity, and debt are consideration that can be used to fund a transaction.

Country Club Deal: n. As opposed to a professional investment firm with committed capital, the hat is passed around the country club by a "deal guy" to round up enough money to close a transaction
Country club deals usually fall apart, either before or after closing, because the organizer is part-time and lightly committed, and the backers are unsophisticated.

Covenants: n. A written promise to act or refrain from acting, depending on conditions
When a bank loans a company money, the loan agreement will include covenants, which may limit the operational choices the company may make.

Drag-Along/Tag-Along Rights: n. A drag-along right is the contractual right of the majority shareholder to force a minority shareholder to join a sale. A tag-along right is the contractual right of a minority shareholder to choose to join a sale by the majority shareholder.
A majority shareholder may exercise drag-along rights. A minority shareholder may exercise tag-along rights. Neither may choose to exercise their rights.

Due Diligence: n. An investigation of a company and its leadership prior to signing a purchase agreement
Buyers use due diligence to validate their understanding. Surprises are the enemy.

Earnout: n. Money that is paid out at a later date (or dates) based on meeting previously agreed upon performance criteria
An earnout presents an opportunity for a seller to receive more than what is paid at close. If a seller expects their company will grow considerably in the next few years, an earnout can be a useful way to earn more, assuming those performance expectations become reality and the buyer is reputable.

Earnest Money: n. A financial commitment, usually non-refundable, paid prior to purchase

Often used in real estate transactions, earnest money is put down to reserve the property while the buyer sorts out financing. Earnest money is unusual for purchases of operating companies.

EBIT: n. Earnings before interest and taxes
EBIT provides a rough estimate of the company's profitability before taxes.

EBITDA: n. Earnings before interest, taxes, depreciation, and amortization
EBITDA is commonly used as an approximation for cash flow because it takes many of the financing and investment decisions out of the mix, providing a way to compare dissimilar companies. However, as Charlie Munger said, "EBITDA is B.S. earnings."

Enterprise Value: n. The investor's appraisal of the company's current value, usually based on a multiple of earnings or valuation of assets
When someone says, "I got $15 million for my business," they are usually referring to the enterprise value, not the cash at close. The enterprise value can be deceiving, as it must be broken down into cash at close, equity rollover, payments over time, and other uses of cash to determine actual proceeds to a seller.

Equity: n. Ownership
As a seller, you are selling your equity.

Escrow: n. A third-party account established for the purpose of holding proceeds for a period of time
Money can be placed in escrow to cover future liabilities as agreed upon by the parties.

Family Office: n. A pool of family wealth
A family office may directly invest in a company, but most often invests in professional managers' funds. They will have a net worth rather than a fund. Some

are structured like a private equity firm with active leadership, while others are more passive.

Fund: n. A pool of capital committed for a specific purpose
Limited partners invest in a private equity fund, and general partners use that fund to invest in companies.

Fundless Sponsor: n. An investor or investment group that does not have a pool of committed capital
A fundless sponsor likely knows capital sources, but will have to present and negotiate the opportunity to secure funding.

Guarantee (Personal/Corporate/Limited): n. A promise that obligations will be fulfilled. A personal guarantee is secured by the personal assets of the guarantor. A corporate guarantee is secured by the assets of the corporation. A limited guarantee has limitations that restrict the guarantor's future liability.
Guarantees are tools to shift risk based on pre-agreed upon circumstances.

Indication of Interest (IOI)/Term Sheet: n. A non-binding offer
An IOI tells you a buyer is interested, and what they believe the company is worth, under certain terms. Depending on the prospective buyer, it may include more details, but none of those details are final or guaranteed.

Interest-Only: adj. This refers to a period of time in which no payments will be made on the principal, but interest payments will be made
A term sheet may state the following about a seller note: "Six-year note, with the first three years interest-only." This means that the note will pay interest during the first three years, then fully amortize over the remaining three years.

Intermediary: n. A representative acting on behalf of a seller or a buyer
A good intermediary seeks to create a match between the buyer and the seller.

Letter of Intent (LOI): n. A legal document that acts as an "agreement to agree" on outlined terms, pending due diligence
When you sign an LOI, there is generally an exclusivity clause, which means you will break off communication with other potential buyers and work to close with this particular buyer.

Line of Credit: n. A pre-established pool of debt financing a company may draw upon, as needed, from a bank or other financial institution
A company may tap into a line of credit to cover a short-term working capital need.

Lower Middle Market: n. A segment of private companies, defined as having an enterprise value between $5 million and $100 million
The companies most directly addressed in this book are companies that fall in the lower end of the lower middle market, having enterprise values between $5 million and $50 million.

Mezzanine Debt: n. A type of debt that falls in payoff priority behind senior debt and is typically unsecured, or lightly secured, which extends the borrowing capacity of a buyer, but comes with a high interest rate
A private equity group may choose to employ both senior debt and mezz debt in a deal.

Multiple: n. A multiplier, based on industry and performance criteria, that is applied to either earnings or revenue to determine the value of a company
A company with EBIT of $4 million and a multiple of 4.5X has a valuation of $18 million (4 x 4.5 = 18). Generally, most companies are valued on a multiple of earnings. The exception is software companies with strong recurring revenue, but with little profit, which are commonly valued on a multiple of revenue.

Net Working Capital: n. Equal to a company's current assets less current liabilities, this represents the amount of capital needed to operate the business

A buyer will expect net working capital to be left to operate the business post-close. The amount can be a predetermined figure, or a formula to be calculated at closing.

Non-Disclosure Agreement (NDA)/Confidentiality Agreement (CA): n. A legal contract that outlines information and materials that are considered confidential, and restricts the parties from sharing the confidential data with a third party, use the data apart from the intent in sharing it

A seller can get comfortable sharing detailed information with a prospective buyer by having them sign an NDA first. If the buyer breaks confidentiality after signing the NDA, there are legal consequences.

Non-Owner Management: n. Operators of a company who do not own equity

A buyer will want to understand if there is non-owner management in place, and whether they will be staying with the business post-close, are aware of a potential transaction, and how they are incentivized.

Ongoing Concern: n. A transferable business, which is operating ongoingly and can carry out its commitments, obligations, and objectives

A company is an ongoing concern.

Operating Agreement: n. A legal document that outlines key financial and functional decision-making, and is used to govern operations of the company

As part of the transaction, all remaining equity holders will sign the operating agreement, which outlines who must consent to future decisions.

Option to Purchase: n. As part of a lease agreement, the option gives the tenant the contractual ability to purchase the property
The option to purchase real estate may include a formula by which the value will be assessed (e.g. cap rate), or a process for determining the value (e.g. collection of independent assessments).

Owner Earnings: n. What "sticks" to the owners; the pre-tax net profit of the business as defined by earnings less capital expenditures, operating interest (e.g. interest on line of credit), and active owner normalized compensation
At adventur.es, we base our valuations on a multiple of owner earnings.

Private Equity Group (PEG): n. A firm that invests in private equities, typically investing capital out of a fund
The most common financial buyer is a PEG.

Purchase Agreement: n. A legal document that outlines the terms and conditions of the sale of assets or equity from a seller to a buyer
The company hasn't been sold until both parties sign the purchase agreement and the consideration has been transferred.

Purchase Price Adjustment: n. A change in the amount owed to the seller
If the buyer discovers something in due diligence previously undisclosed, they may request a purchase price adjustment.

Quality of Earnings (Q of E): n. A diagnosis, usually delivered in the form of a report by an accounting firm, detailing a company's underlying financial strength
A buyer may conduct a Q of E analysis as part of due diligence.

Representations & Warranties: n. A representation is an assertion of a fact or circumstance as truthful. A warranty is a promise of indemnity if the assertion proves to be false.

Reps and warranties are outlined in the purchase agreement and share risk between the buyer and seller.

Re-trade: v. The act of re-negotiating the purchase price and/or terms of the deal after they've been agreed upon

A less-than-ethical buyer may get a seller under LOI with the intention of re-trading the deal after dragging the other party through costly and time-consuming due diligence.

Right of First Refusal: n. A right by one party to purchase something from a second party before the second party may sell the asset to a third party

A majority owner typically has a right of first refusal on all minority share-holders' equity.

Rollover: n. The amount of equity a seller continues to own post-transaction

If a seller chooses to sell some of their shares, the amount that remains is "rolled over" into the new ownership structure.

Search Fund: n. Typically launched by recent MBA graduates and operating for two years in search of a company to acquire

Like fundless sponsors, search funds do not have committed capital, and are likely to be led by younger operators looking to install themselves as the day-to-day leader of the business post-close.

Seller Note: n. Seller-funded debt

Buyers like a seller note because it aligns the seller's interests and provides some financial leverage.

Seller's Discretionary Earnings (SDE): n. Pre-tax net earnings that flow to the owner, including their compensation and benefits, and excluding any one-time expenses and unrelated revenue or expenses
Smaller businesses (under $5 million in enterprise value) may be valued on a multiple of SDE, because the buyer will typically operate the company post-close.

Senior Debt: n. Debt that takes priority over other repayment obligations
Senior debt is typically provided by banks and requires strict covenants to be maintained, including the repayment schedule.

Site Visit: n. When a buyer visits a seller, usually including a tour of operations, followed by an off-site discussion and a meal
Most buyers will conduct a site visit before drafting an LOI.

Subordination: n. The condition of being lower in priority repayment
In the case of debt, seller notes are usually subordinate to all other debt, and mezz debt is subordinate to bank debt. Bank debt is rarely subordinate to anything else — they get paid first.

Triple Net Lease: n. A lease agreement in which the tenant agrees to pay for all real estate taxes, maintenance, and insurance, in addition to rent, utilities, etc.
Most buildings are leased on a triple net basis.

Abbreviations

BATNA: Best alternative to a negotiated agreement

CA: Confidentiality agreement

CIM: Confidential information memorandum

EBIT: Earnings before interest and taxes

EBITDA: Earnings before interest, taxes, depreciation, and amortization

ESOP: Employee stock ownership plan

GAAP: Generally accepted accounting principles

GP: General partner

IOI: Indication of interest

IP: Intellectual property

IRR: Internal rate of return

KPI: Key performance indicator

LOI: Letter of intent

LP: Limited partner

M&A: Mergers & acquisitions

NNN: Triple-net

NDA: Non-disclosure agreement

OPM: Other people's money

PEG: Private equity group

Q of E: Quality of earnings

ROA: Return on assets

ROE: Return on equity

TTM: Trailing twelve months

APPENDIX B
A PROFESSIONAL COLONOSCOPY:
Due Diligence Details

Due diligence is a grueling process, and intentionally so. No one sane is going to pay millions of dollars for something they have not verified to be valuable. That is the purpose of due diligence.

The purpose of this appendix is to expose you, as a seller, to what document requests and questions will likely be asked of you throughout the process. It's long. It's detailed. It likely looks intimidating. As stated throughout the book, the reality is selling a company is hard. But the result is worth it.

The Documents

Below is a list of documents commonly prepared and/or exchanged between the parties throughout the due diligence process:

- Non-Disclosure/Confidentiality Agreement
- Purchase Agreement
- Note for Seller Financing
- Financial Statements for the Current and Past 2 to 3 Years
- Statement of Seller's Discretionary Earnings or Cash Flow

- Financial Ratios and Trends
- Accounts Payable and Accounts Receivables Aging Reports
- Inventory List with Value Detail
- List of Fixtures, Furnishings and Equipment with Value Detail
- Asset Depreciation Schedule from Tax Return
- Supplier and Distributor Contracts
- Client List and Major Client Contracts
- Staffing List with Hire Dates and Salaries; Employment Agreements
- Organizational Chart
- Photos of Business
- List of Opportunities for Improvement with Revenue/Profit Projections for Each
- Business Formation Documents
- Corporate or Schedule C Tax Returns for Past 2 to 3 Years
- Building or Office Leases
- Equipment Leases and Maintenance Agreements
- Business Licenses, Certifications and Registrations
- Professional Certificates
- Insurance Policies
- Copies Proving Ownership of Patents, Trademarks and Other Intellectual Property
- Outstanding Loan Agreements
- Description of Liens
- Product/Service Descriptions and Price Lists
- Marketing Plan and Samples of Marketing Materials
- Employment Manual

The Question List

"If one could open the lid, so to speak, and see what was in the head of the experienced decision maker, one would find that he had at his disposal repertoires of possible actions; that he had checklists of things to think about before he acted."
—Herbert Simon, American economist

The following pages provide a list of due diligence questions we typically use at adventur.es. There are questions specific to industries and types of transactions that are excluded, but this list will provide a general idea of what types of requests and questions to expect.

The Company

Corporation

- Please provide the Company's Articles of Incorporation and bylaws, as amended to date.
- Please provide the minutes of the meetings of the Board of Directors of the Company and any committees thereof, and of the stockholders of the Company, and copies of written consents in lieu of such meetings, for the previous five years (hereinafter referred to as the "Historical Period").
- Please provide all materials prepared for distribution to shareholders or directors during the Historical Period.
- Please provide a list of jurisdictions in which the Company is qualified to do business as a foreign corporation.
- Please provide a schedule of all states and countries in which the Company has offices, plants, employees, or representatives or in which the Company has annual sales of at least $500,000.
- Has the Company ever done business, or is it currently doing business, under a name other than [Name]?

- Does the Company now, or has it ever, owned an interest in any other enterprise? If so, please provide relevant details and documentation.
- If applicable, please provide any management and investment studies or reports of the Company, including any valuations and appraisals of the Company or any of its divisions, undertaken during the Historical period.
- Please provide any brochures and reports used during the Historical Period to describe the Company and its products.
- Please provide an updated organizational chart depicting the Company hierarchy, including employee names and titles and notes regarding any planned retirement transitions. Furthermore, please indicate if any employees are classified as part-time or temporary employees.
- Please provide all Company policy manuals and written descriptions of all unwritten Company policies, including but not limited to copies of all codes of ethics/conduct, whistleblower policies, document retention policies, and other material corporate governance policies and procedures.
- Please provide all reasonably available press clippings and press releases relating to the Company for the past three years.
- Is the Company a member of any industry associations? If so, please list, including length of tenure and associated cost.
- Please provide any documents relating to the Company's status as an approved vendor to any party, and evidencing quality awards or designations.
- Please provide a list of all transactions or business relationships of the Company with any subsidiary, parent, or affiliate including, but not limited to (a) borrowing arrangements or other credit arrangements; (b) joint or shared activities including purchasing, marketing, sales, common offices, or common management; and (c) staff or other services provided. For each such relationship,

provide copies of agreements or other written descriptions of such arrangements, together with fee schedules and amounts involved for each of the last five years.

- Please provide a schedule of all whistleblower complaints made during the Historical Period and actions taken with respect to such complaints.
- Please provide copies of all corporate governance committee charters, if applicable.
- Please provide the stock transfer ledger of the Company and copies of stock certificates of the Company.

Contracts

- Please provide all standard form contracts used by the Company (and any material third-party form used) including, but not limited to warranty agreements or terms, purchase orders, invoices, vendor and customer agreements.
- Please provide all material contracts with customers and suppliers.
- Is the Company a party to any joint venture agreement, partnership agreement, or agreement involving a sharing of profits or technology of the Company? If so, please provide them for review.
- Please provide a schedule of any transactions (including purchase, sale, financing or loan agreements) between the Company and any shareholder, officer, director, employee, or affiliate of the Company (including spouses, children, and other relatives of any affiliates thereof), and copies of all documents relating to such transactions.
- Is the Company a party to any non-competition, standstill, or confidentiality agreement? Is it a party to any other agreement

limiting its ability to engage in business anywhere in the world? If so, please provide all such agreements for review.

- Is the Company a party to any exclusivity agreement? If so, please provide the agreement for review.

- Is the Company involved in any agreement or contract for which it or another party is in default, or which is in the process of being terminated or modified? If so, please provide a copy of the agreement or contract and a brief description of the circumstances that led to the default, modification, or termination.

- Please provide a copy of any contract or agreement to which the Company is a party which contains a change of control or assignment provision.

- Please provide any professional service agreements to which the Company is a party.

- Please provide all contracts relating to the sale of any significant Company asset or property, other than inventory in the ordinary course of business.

- Please provide a list and brief description of any guarantee of the obligations of the Company's customers, suppliers, officers, directors, employees, or others.

- Is the Company a party to any distribution, dealer, sales agency, advertising or consignment agreement? If so, please provide all such agreements for review.

- Please provide details and available documentation relating to any note, instrument, agreement, mortgage, lease, license, franchise, governmental permit or judgment, order, or decree which involves covenants or other restrictions which could be violated or triggered by an acquisition of the Company or any of its assets.

- Is the Company a party to any agreements or instruments which place restrictions or encumbrances on assets of the Company (including rights of first refusal or other preferential rights regarding the sale of Company assets, security agreements, and judicial or administrative orders or decrees)? If so, please provide all such agreements or instruments for review.

- Please provide purchase or lease agreements for machinery, equipment, or other personal property currently used to operate the business.
- Please provide copies of any licenses to which the Company is a party, including software licenses.
- Is the Company a party to any powers of attorney, agency, or representation agreements? If so, please provide them for review.
- Is the Company a party to any logistics contracts or warehouse management agreements? If so, please provide them for review.
- Is the Company involved with any third party in joint marketing, development or distribution efforts? If so, please describe the circumstances and reasoning behind such joint efforts, and any agreements (written or oral) relating thereto.
- Please provide written summaries of any oral agreements between the Company and any other person.
- Please provide copies of any contracts not entered into in the ordinary course of business.
- Please provide a schedule and copies of any agreements that may restrict the Company's activities in any significant manner and that were not provided pursuant to any of the previous questions.

Capitalization

- Please provide all governmental permits, notices of exemption, and consents for issuance or transfer of the Company's securities and evidence of qualification or exemption under applicable blue sky laws.
- Please provide a list of all securities owned by the Company.

- Has any person other than the current owner ever made a claim asserting a right to an equity interest in the Company? If so, please provide a comprehensive description of the situation and its resolution.
- Please briefly describe any agreements with any broker, finder, or other person or entity relating to the past, present, or proposed offering of securities.
- Are there any agreements between the Company and its sole shareholder regarding management or control of the Company?

Operations

- What is the total market size for the Company's products?
- How does management expect the market for its products to change in the next five years?
- Please prepare a list of major competitors and describe the level of competition (e.g. in what geographic area do they operate? Could their products act as a substitute for those sold by Company?)
- Please provide an assessment of the relative market share of the Company and its major competitors.
- Please describe the Company's existing marketing strategy and any contemplated changes.
- To the extent that it exists, please provide any current and historical market research and customer surveys regarding geographic expansion opportunities or new product development.
- For each individual facility, please list the production capacities and discuss current utilization of capacity (e.g. percent of capacity used, number of shifts, number of hours per shift, etc.).
- Are there any current plans to acquire or divest any material assets, including plans to build or acquire new facilities? If so, please provide a description of such plans.

- Please provide a current price list for all products sold, together with methodology, assumptions, analysis, and build up related to the determination of product pricing.
- Please describe any planned product lines or services that are not currently in existence.
- Please describe the Company's collection process and the terms extended.
- Please provide copies of all advertising and promotional materials published in print or online for the most recent two years, and for email campaigns utilized during the TTM period.
- Please provide a description of any marketing agency relationships utilized during the Historical Period.
- Please list and describe any marketing restrictions currently applicable to the Company.
- Please provide Google Analytics statistics for the Company's website for the previous two years and the TTM period.
- Please describe the size and scope of the Company's email list, as well as the last time it was scrubbed.
- Please provide descriptions of all warranties available to customers for the previous two years and the TTM period.
- Please provide a list and summary description of all warranty claims for the Historical Period.
- Please provide a list and summary description of all product liability claims for the Historical Period.
- Please provide a list of all bank accounts maintained by the Company, including name of bank, bank officer, type of accounts, name and number of account, and any authorized signers on the account.
- Please provide a schedule of the Company's twenty largest customers for each of the last three years, including the amount sold annually, and a description of any discounts or special payment terms offered.

- Please provide a schedule of the Company's twenty largest suppliers/vendors, setting forth annual amounts purchased, and a summary description of each supply arrangement (e.g., pursuant to a written contract or through another arrangement). For those supply arrangements governed by a written contract, please provide copies of such contracts.
- Please provide a list of all material assets owned by the Company.

Insurance

- Please provide a list of insurance coverages in force (e.g., business interruption, directors and officers, fire or casualty, extended coverage, general liability, key man, motor vehicle, professional liability, product liability, unemployment compensation, etc.), including names of carriers, brokers, description of coverage, amounts of coverage, amounts of premiums, expiration dates, and significant conditions and benefits.
- Please describe any circumstances that currently exist that could foreseeably lead to the Company making a claim in the future.
- Please provide copies of any insurance analyses or reports prepared for the Company.
- Please provide a schedule of loss and claims experience for the Historical Period, and any correspondence relating thereto.
- Please provide a description of areas in which the Company is self-insured, and methods of self-insurance.
- Please describe any potential uninsured or underinsured liabilities.
- Please provide copies of cover sheets of insurance policies and binders.
- Please provide an analysis of worker's compensation coverage and claims experience for the Historical Period.

- Please describe any changes in insurance coverages during the Historical Period.
- Please provide copies of any actuarial evaluations.

Financial Information

Accounting

- Please provide the most recent interim financial statements available, as well as the complete financial statements for each year of the Historical Period.
- Which accounting personnel and management members should we speak with to gain an understanding of the operations and the accounting, reporting, and control systems?
- Please summarize any significant accounting policies not described in the Confidential Information Memorandum, including judgmental reserves and estimates.
- Have there been any changes in accounting practices or policies during the Historical Period? If so, what are the changes and why were they made?
- Please provide any material correspondence from the Company's outside tax advisors and accountants received during the Historical Period regarding the Company's accounting controls, methods of accounting, and other procedures.
- Please identify the scope, audit procedures, control issues, accounting policies, etc., relating to the most recent external audit of the Company. Please include copies of any reports made by the external auditor and delivered to the Company.
- Has an external auditor evaluated the Company's procedures related to contract accounting at any point during the Historical Period? If so, please provide the auditor's findings and conclusions.

- Review any non-GAAP financial measures used in public documents, accompanied by the most directly comparable GAAP financial measure and reconciliation to GAAP, along with reasons for use of non-GAAP measures.

Financial Matters

- Please provide copies of any management letters issued by the Company's outside accountants for the last five years, to the extent any such letters exist.
- Please provide historical sales data for the Historical Period.
- Please provide a copy of your most recently prepared budget.
- Please describe any discounts (or patterns of discounts) given to customers during the Historical Period and the Company's reasoning for providing such discounts.
- Please describe any discounts received from suppliers during the Historical Period and the terms upon which the discount was based.
- Please explain how the Company's method of accounting for inventory impacts the cost of goods sold figure.
- Please explain any noticeable trends in major categories of costs over the last two (2) years and TTM period.
- Please provide details about the Company's recurring sales-related costs other than labor and product costs.
- Please describe the trends in the major categories of controllable expenses over the last two years and TTM period (i.e. direct operating expenses, advertising and promotions, utilities, general and administrative, repairs and maintenance, supplies, etc.).
- Please describe the trends in the major categories of non-controllable expenses over the last two years and TTM period (i.e. rent, property taxes, property insurance, G&A costs, etc.).

- Please provide a list of significant third party suppliers along with the amount of product (in dollar terms) purchased from them in the TTM period.
- Please explain the major drivers for significant components of costs (salaries, insurance, rent, utilities, etc.).
- Please list any outsourced services and describe the relationship with and capacity of these service providers.
- Please describe the difference between procedures performed at the home office vs. at the other locations.
- Are any costs for services performed by the home office allocated to other offices?
- Please provide copies of all written investment policies of the Company.
- Please provide the corporate bank reconciliation as of the latest balance sheet date.
- Please describe, in detail, the receivable system and controls, walking through a standard transaction through the sales, billing, accounts receivable, and collections cycle.
- Please provide claims collection rates for the previous two years and the TTM period.
- Please provide any aged AR trial balances for the previous two years and the TTM period.
- Has the Company entered into a factoring relationship during the Historical Period? If so, please describe the arrangement and the fees incurred.

Taxes

- Please provide copies of all federal, state, local, and foreign tax returns (as applicable) for the last five years, including sales, property, franchise, payroll, excise, withholding and capital tax returns, and consolidated returns (if any) of the Company.

- Please provide a list of any pending tax matters, including, but not limited to, audits, extensions of time, waivers of statutes of limitations, and deficiency/assessments, and the status of any outstanding tax audits, including a list of all audit adjustments proposed by any taxing authority.
- Please provide copies of all communications and agreements between the Company and any taxing authority for the Historical Period.
- Please describe any preferred tax status or tax benefit which may be adversely affected by the proposed acquisition and any related transactions, including a summary of any available tax attribute carry-forwards.
- Please provide a list of tax years open and indicate whether the IRS or any other taxing authority has indicated that a claim may be asserted with respect thereto.
- Please provide audit and revenue agents' reports (federal, state, and local) for the Historical Period.
- Please provide any tax settlement documents and correspondence for the Historical Period.
- Please provide copies of any agreements waiving statute of limitations or extending time for filing tax returns.
- Please provide copies of any material tax opinions and rulings.
- Please provide evidence that all payroll, withholding, sales, use, franchise, and real and personal property taxes are paid.
- If applicable, please provide evidence that the Company has paid all transfer taxes related to the sale of personal or real property for the Historical Period.
- Please describe any tax sharing, tax allocation, or related intercompany agreements, if applicable.
- Please provide details regarding the Company's unemployment tax rate and payment status.
- Please describe any tax abatement or incentive agreements.

- Does the Company have any outstanding tax elections?

Assets & Liabilities

Inventory

- Please give a detailed description of the Company's inventory costing system.
- How often does the Company take physical inventories, and is inventory ever deemed obsolete? If so, what method does the Company use to determine obsolete inventory?
- Please provide information regarding inventory turnover rates.
- Please provide listings of historical book-to-physical adjustments for the last two fiscal years.
- Please provide a schedule of any write-down of the value of any inventory or write-off as uncollectible of any notes or accounts receivable made by the Company during the Historical Period, other than immaterial write-downs or write-offs in the ordinary course of business.
- Please describe the Company's accounting for inventory reserves, if any, and the effect on current periods' earnings.

Fixed Assets

- Please provide a list of all material assets owned by the Company.
- Please provide a copy of the most recent fixed asset register.
- Please provide a dated copy of latest physical inventory of all equipment and other assets.
- Please list and briefly explain capital expenditures made in the last two fiscal years and TTM period as well as projected capital expenditure assumptions.

- Please explain the depreciation policies and methods adopted for each asset class.
- Please prepare a legal description of all properties owned or utilized by the Company.
- Please provide a copy of most recent aged accounts receivable and aged accounts payable reports.
- Please describe the Company's capitalization policy.
- Please provide a detailed description of any off-balance sheet arrangements, liabilities, or obligations of any nature (fixed or contingent, matured or unmatured) that are not shown or otherwise provided for in the Company's current financial statements. Explain (i) the nature and purpose of any such off-balance sheet arrangements; (ii) the importance to the Company of such arrangements; (iii) the amounts of revenue, expenses, and cash flows arising from such arrangements; (iv) any known event, demand, commitment, trend, or uncertainty that is reasonably likely to result in the termination of the arrangement (or reduction in availability to the Company) and the course of action the Company has taken or proposes to take in response to such circumstances.

Leases & Debt

- What are the key terms for leasing the leased real estate?
- Are there any leased assets other than the leased real estate?
- Please provide copies of all significant lease agreements.
- Please provide all material correspondence with lenders of the Company during the last three years including all compliance reports submitted by the Company or its independent public accountants during the last three years.
- Please provide any leases of personal property, security agreements, UCC-1 financing statement filings, indentures,

guarantees, installment purchase agreements, letters of credit, and financing leases.

- Please list all encumbrances and restrictions affecting Company assets and property.
- Please provide a detailed description of any bad debts and agreements or arrangements that are expected to result in a loss.
- Please provide a list and description of any contingent liabilities not disclosed or described in financial statements.
- Please list any debit, large or old outstanding balances.
- Please provide a list of general accrued liabilities (i.e. identifiable operating liabilities).
- Does the Company engage in any 'off-the-books' activities? If so, please give a detailed description of the activities.
- Please provide a written summary of the policies related to accounting for worker's compensation, product warranties, and group insurance.
- Please describe all (i) the monetary reserves established for specific risk situations and (ii) disagreements with the Company's outside auditors concerning the Company's financial reporting, including those arising from contracts and agreements, price redetermination or renegotiation, unfunded pension plan liability, antitrust matters, or environmental matters.
- Please provide a list of capital expenditures exceeding $10,000 made during the Historical Period and describe any planned or contemplated capital expenditures exceeding that amount. Include along with the list any contracts related to any such capital expenditures.
- Does the Company utilize any capitalized software? If so, describe its value and related amortization schedule.
- Please provide a schedule of currently outstanding short-term debt, long-term debt, intercompany debt, contingent obligations, and capital lease obligations of the Company, including amounts,

maturities, balances due, interest rates, and prepayment terms, together with copies of material correspondence to/from lenders during prior 12 months and compliance reports prepared by the Company or its auditors.

- Please provide copies of all agreements evidencing borrowings by the Company, whether secured or unsecured, documented or undocumented, including loan and credit agreements, mortgages, deeds of trust, letters of credit, indentures, promissory notes, and other evidences of indebtedness, and any amendments, renewals, notices or waivers.
- Is the Company a party to any financing agreements with or for suppliers or customers? If so, please provide copies of such agreements.
- Please provide copies of all documents and agreements evidencing other material financing arrangements, including capital leases, synthetic leases, sale and leaseback arrangements, installment purchases, or similar agreements.
- Please provide copies of all agreements pursuant to which the Company is or will be subject to any obligation to provide funds to or to make investments in any other person (in the form of a loan, capital contribution, or otherwise).
- Please provide a list of outstanding standby letters of credit, performance bonds, performance guarantees, and similar credit support obligations (including, without limitation, copies of all letters of credit outstanding under the senior revolving credit facility and the underlying agreement(s) requiring the Company to provide such credit support).
- Please provide copies of any currently outstanding commitment letters or other correspondence relating to proposed financing or borrowings which may involve amounts in excess of $50,000 of indebtedness of the Company.

- Please provide a schedule of any liabilities retained in connection with the divestiture of assets or operations during the Historical Period. For any such liabilities, include any available documentation relating to any such divestiture.

Human Resources

Personnel

- Please provide a schedule of the names of:
  - Current officers and directors and other key employees (and a brief description for each); and
  - Any officers and directors and other key employees who have recently resigned or been terminated and all compensation paid during the last five fiscal years to the same, including base salary, bonus program (if any), benefits, prerequisites, and length of service.
- For each director, please indicate whether they are an independent director and disclose their length of service on the Board of Directors.
- For each employee listed on the organizational chart, please provide base salary, bonus potential, and all benefits.
- Please provide copies of all contracts or agreements with temporary employees.
- Please provide copies of any management and service agreements, employee collective bargaining agreements, employment agreements, deferred compensation agreements or arrangements, severance agreements or arrangements, and consulting agreements, including a description of any oral agreements.
- Please provide a list of any involvement of officers, directors, and employees in criminal proceedings and significant civil litigation.

- Please provide any effective indemnification agreements with officers and directors.
- Please provide a schedule of all loans made by or to the Company to or from any officer, director, employee, or shareholder, and copies of all related documents.
- Please provide any current employee manuals, employee handbooks, relations policies, programs, practices, agreements, procedures, or other employment policies or terms and conditions of employment, including any unwritten policies.
- Please provide a schedule of any prior, pending or threatened (a) unfair labor practice charge or complaint against the Company before the National Labor Relations Board (NLRB), Equal Employment Opportunity Commission (EEOC), Occupational Health and Safety Association (OSHA), State Workers' Compensation Agencies or any other federal, state or foreign labor relations board, (b) employee grievance against the Company, (c) arbitration proceeding against the Company, and (d) any other employee claims against the Company.
- Please provide a schedule of all worker's compensation claims experienced by the Company in the last two years showing (a) the amounts paid to date in respect thereof, (b) the current status of such claims, and (c) the amounts, if any, reserved for such claims.
- Please provide a schedule of any bonus or special compensation granted or increase in compensation or benefits payable to any directors, officers, or employees of the Company for the prior three years.
- Has there been any labor union organizing activity in the last five years? If so, please describe the circumstances surrounding such activity and its resolution.
- Please provide a listing of management employees through department head with experience, responsibilities, years with

the Company, and compensation (including salary, bonus and fringe benefits).

- Please provide a listing of the number of employees by category, location, and department.
- Please provide employee turnover statistics for the Historical Period.
- If applicable, provide a schedule of all loans to employees and copies of all related documents.
- Please provide a list of all independent contractors that have performed work on behalf of the Company in the prior two years, and copies of all agreements relating to such contractors.
- Please describe any material labor disputes, strikes, or work stoppages which have occurred during the Historical Period.
- Please provide absenteeism, disciplinary actions, accident records, and turnover rates of employees the Company.
- Please provide copies of any special compensation or retention arrangements in connection with the proposed transaction, other than those that have already been disclosed.
- Please provide employee offer letters and reviews.

Payroll & Benefits

- Please provide a schedule of total employee costs for the previous two fiscal years as well as payroll reports for that same period.
- Please provide a schedule of compensation paid to key management and sales personnel over the Historical Period (other than that already disclosed).
- Please describe the trends in the major categories of Labor and Benefits over the last two years and the TTM period (i.e. direct operating labor, payroll taxes, and employer benefits).
- Please explain the basis (cash or accrual) for recording benefit costs and liabilities.

- Please describe benefit packages available to employees (i.e., length of time before receiving benefits, management and administrative benefits, fringe benefits, commissions, and bonuses).
- Please provide copies of any bonus, pension, profit sharing, or annuity plans affecting the compensation of officers, directors, and employees in effect during any portion of the last three years.
- Please describe any thrift, performance, bonus, incentive, retirement, welfare, hospitalization, disability, life, or other insurance plans or programs available to employees and any other employee benefit plan, program, agreement, or arrangement.
- Please provide any administrative service agreements (or other agreements with benefit plan administrators) with respect to any benefit plans.
- With respect to each pension plan:
  - Provide plan and pension trust instruments;
  - Provide plan summaries (handouts for employee participants);
  - Provide financial statements and plan evaluations for the last plan year;
  - Provide the most recent actuarial reports;
  - Provide copies of IRS Forms 5500 for each plan for the last three years;
  - Provide copies of any and all IRS determination letters; and
  - Describe cost benefit information for the most recent plan year, including administrative costs, employer contributions, employee contributions, and benefit distributions.
- Please provide a description of all severance policies (including any written materials).

- Please provide a description and itemized schedule of all non-salary "perks" offered to officers, directors, and employees.
- Please provide any notices or other communications issued during the Historical Period relating to blackout periods under any defined contribution plan or regarding any further reductions in medical, pension, or other employee benefit or regarding the termination of any employee benefit arrangements.
- Has the Company participated in any multi-employer or multiple employer plans to which it has or had in the past an obligation to contribute, including pension or welfare funds? If so, please provide a list of such plans together with copies of all contracts and agreements related to the same.
- Please provide copies of the most recent report regarding post-retirement liabilities prepared in accordance with FASB and a schedule of life and/or health benefits for retired employees or dependents indicating whether liability for those benefits has been determined, whether and how these benefits have been funded, and the number of retirees receiving benefits.
- Please provide copies of all agreements relating to "rabbi trusts" or other arrangements securing in any way the payment of deferred compensation, severance, or other payments to employees or directors.

Facilities/Real Estate

Real Estate

- For all facilities (offices, warehouses, etc.) currently utilized by the Company, please provide details regarding its age, type of construction, amount of floor space, and estimated remaining life.
- For all leased real property, and any real property owned by the Company and leased to any third party, please provide a

description of the lessor and a list of any leasehold improvements including information regarding cost, depreciated value, and ownership of such improvements.

- Please provide all contracts for the purchase, sale, or lease of real property, or any option to purchase or sell real property, or any management contract relating to real property to which the Company is a party or by which it is bound.
- Please provide a description of mortgages, liens, pledges, and encumbrances regarding any assets to which one or more of those categories apply.
- Please provide copies of all agreements affecting real property.
- Please provide copies of all certificates of occupancy and estoppel certificates applicable to the company.
- To the extent that they exist, please provide copies of any engineering reports or studies regarding any facility utilized by the Company.
- Please provide a list of security deposits held or paid.
- Please provide a schedule of all easements and rights-of-way required for operation of the business, including a brief description of why each is necessary.
- Please provide a schedule of any continuing obligations under expired leases or agreements relating to the sale of real property by the Company or any predecessor entities.
- Please provide a description of any zoning status and variances related to all real property utilized by the Company, as well as any unresolved notices of violation of zoning requirements or land-use restrictions.

Environmental

- Please provide a list of all environmental permits and permit applications of the Company, together with copies of related correspondence and consideration of transferability.
- Please list any materials used in operation of the business that are subject to environmental regulation at the federal, state, or local level.
- Please provide a description of the condition of neighboring areas (landfills, Superfund or Part 201 sites, spills, relations with neighbors, common drainage of waste treatment areas).
- Please provide a list of former Company properties and properties formerly owned or operated by the Company. With respect to current or former Company properties or properties formerly owned or operated, provide evidence of chain of title for at least the last 50 years.
- Review all information and correspondence regarding compliance with federal, state, local, or foreign environmental laws and regulations (including, without limitation, permits, permit applications, notices of violation, compliance orders and agreements, pollution control capital expenditure reports, and information relating to the presence of UST's, PCB's, or asbestos).
- Review all information and correspondence regarding generation, treatment, storage, and disposition of hazardous substances (including, without limitation, permits, spill reports and notifications, manifests, financial estimates and reserves for environmental liabilities, and a list of on-site and off-site waste disposal sites).
- Examine all internal Company reports concerning environmental matters relating to current or former Company properties or properties formerly owned or operated.

- Review all material documents relating to regulatory proceedings (including, without limitation, information requests under CERCLA, 104(e) and similar federal, state, local or foreign laws or regulations).
- Examine copies of all other environmental studies and surveys, including any Phase I or Phase II reports.
- Examine copies of all notices, complaints (whether formal or informal), suits or similar documents sent to, received by or served upon the Company by any environmental regulatory or protective agency, whether federal, state, or local.
- Review a description of any past or ongoing remediation efforts.
- Review regulatory lists and files (state records, National Priority List, state policy, fire marshal underground storage tank records, etc.).
- Obtain copies of all waste manifests related to real estate for which Company has environmental responsibility.

Legal

Legal/Litigation

- Please provide all documentation relating to and description of all pending, threatened, or completed litigation, claims, suits and proceedings in which the Company is, was or could be a defendant for the Historical Period, including the nature of the litigation, the amount involved, any pleadings or substantive filings, and any opinion of counsel as to the probable outcome.
- Please provide any patent, trade secret, non-disclosure, confidentiality, non-compete, and non-solicitation agreements to which the Company is a party and which are currently in effect.
- Please provide a schedule of fines and penalties incurred by the Company during the Historical Period arising out of the operation

of their facilities or equipment, the sale of their products, or the provision of their services.

- To the extent known, please provide details of any other material judgments, injunctions, consent decrees, or cease and desist orders affecting the industry of which the Company is part.

- Please provide all reports to the Company's Board of Directors, or equivalent managing body, from attorneys, appraisers, or others during the Historical Period regarding unsafe, questionable, or illegal matters or practices of the Company.

- Please provide all letters from the Company's auditors to management, auditors' inquiry letters, and all replies to the foregoing for the Historical Period.

- Please provide a description by project of all work performed by outside law firms during the Historical Period.

- Please provide a schedule of all laws, regulations, rules, ordinances, injunctions, franchises, or court orders in respect of which the Company is not in compliance or has received notice of a possible violation.

- Please provide copies of any consent decrees, judgments, other decrees or orders, settlement agreements, and other agreements to which the Company is a party or by which it is bound requiring or prohibiting any future action.

- Please provide copies of all reports, notices, or correspondence relating to any violation or infringement by the Company of government regulations, including any regulations relating to occupational safety and health.

- Please provide copies of letters from lawyers to accountants concerning litigation and other legal proceedings, including all attorney audit letters for the Historical Period.

- Please provide copies of all correspondence with state or federal governmental agencies during the Historical Period.

- Please provide copies of all reports of any regulatory body that has audited or reviewed the Company.
- If applicable, please provide copies of all lobbying registration or disclosure filings with any governmental entity.
- Please provide detailed information regarding any bankruptcy, receivership, or similar proceedings with respect to the Company or its officers or directors.
- Please provide a schedule of all material licenses, permits, registrations, governmental approvals, and clearances obtained, pending, or otherwise required for the conduct of the business of the Company.
- Please provide a schedule of material laws, regulations, rules, ordinances, injunctions, franchises, or court orders that directly impact how the company operates, the status of compliance with respect to each, and a description of all programs, presentations, guidelines, policies, or similar documents relating to the Company's compliance with the laws and regulations of any governmental entity.
- Please provide a summary of all material governmental agency inquiries, citations, notices of violation, fines, or penalties (if any), whether written or oral and including any threatened formal or informal actions or inquiries.

Intellectual Property

- Please provide a list of all domain names owned or utilized by the Company.
- Please provide a schedule including copies of all technology, inventions, patents, patent applications, utility models, designs, trademarks, service marks, trade names, and copyrights, whether registered, unregistered, or the subject of a pending application owned by the Company or in which the Company holds any

right, license, or interest, (hereinafter, 'Company Intellectual Property') showing with respect to each: (a) the product, device, process, service, or business covered thereby; (b) the registered or other owner; and (c) in the case of any of the foregoing not owned by the Company, a brief description of the nature of the right, license or interest of the Company.

- Please provide copies of all documents, information, or other materials pertaining to the application or registration of the Company Intellectual Property both at the state and federal levels.
- Please provide a list and copies of any intellectual property searches or any clearance, availability, validity, or other opinions concerning Company Intellectual Property.
- Please provide a list and copies of all agreements involving the licensing, assigning, or granting of any security interest or other right or ownership interest in any Company Intellectual Property rights to a third party.
- Please provide a list and copies of all agreements involving the licensing, assigning, or granting of any security interest or other right or ownership interest to the Company in a third party's intellectual property rights.
- Please provide a schedule including a list and copies of all documents and other information or materials related to any charges of intellectual property infringement or any other intellectual property dispute made against the Company. For any resolved disputes, please provide a brief description of the resolution.
- Please provide copies of any royalty agreements (whether the Company pays or receives the royalty), if any such agreements exist.
- Please provide a summary of research and development expenditures over the Historical Period.

- Please describe any significant new products, technologies, or processes currently under development.
- Please provide a summary of significant computer software acquired or utilized by the Company and copies of related purchasing, licensing, and other agreements or documents.
- Please provide a summary of any other third party intellectual property used by the Company and any related documents and agreements.
- Please provide copies of agreements (or, for all that are substantially similar, a standard form of the agreement) with employees regarding assignment of intellectual property and confidentiality, along with a description of the Company's policy as to which employees and consultants are required to execute such agreements, and confirmation that the Company has, as a general matter, complied with such policy.
- Please provide a description of and documentation relating to any dispute regarding intellectual property rights that occurred during the Historical Period or is still ongoing. If any of the disputes involved employees or consultants of the Company, please indicate that in the description of the dispute.
- Please provide copies of all nondisclosure or any other agreements restricting disclosure, sharing, or other dissemination of intellectual property to which the Company is a party.
- Please provide a listing and copies of all consent or other agreements involving any of the Company's intellectual property rights not already disclosed pursuant to the above requests.
- If applicable, please provide opinions for patents including right to use, patentability, blocking patents, infringement, and validity.
- Please provide any opinions for trademarks, including those regarding registrability and infringement.
- Please provide documents relating to third-party development and/or testing of the Company's products, services, and/

or proprietary products/information, including third party certifications or testing.

- Please provide copies of all legal opinions, 'cease and desist' letters, or other communications relating to alleged or actual Intellectual Property infringement.
- Please provide a list of all Company uses of the copyright notice.
- Please describe all patent and trademark proceedings and other administrative proceedings in the U.S. Patent and Trademark Office involving the Company (including, for example, opposition proceedings, cancellation proceedings), as well as any consents, judgments, settlements, or decrees relating to same.
- Please provide a schedule of all trade secrets and descriptions thereof, together with a list of third party claims with respect to the same and a description of procedures used to protect trade secrets.
- Please list and provide a brief description of all material pending, threatened and resolved claims, disputes, suits, actions, litigations, or proceedings concerning the value, validity, enforceability, ownership, registration, infringement, or use of any Company Intellectual Property or alleged infringement of any third party intellectual property that have not already been disclosed pursuant to the above requests.

Information Technology

- Please provide a schedule of all IT assets owned or leased by the Company, including PCs, servers, telephones, and other general telecommunications equipment (e.g. PBXs, routers, and switches).
- Please describe the applications used to run the Company's business and support important internal departments and functions including, but not limited to: (i) human resources;

(ii) finance; (iii) customer service; (iv) product provisioning; (v) email / fax / mobile devices; and (vi) intranet.

- Please describe the technological infrastructure, including servers, network and data centers, which are used to run the Company and support important internal departments and functions.
- Please describe how the technologies used by the Company are supported including, but not limited to, helpdesk, application support, and infrastructure support.
- Please describe how the management and maintenance of software and hardware assets is performed.
- Please provide a list of all deployed software, the cost of all such software, and copies of any invoices related to such software.
- Please describe the internal authentication security mechanism (Active Directory, etc.) for regular office use, development, and remote access.
- Please describe what metrics are tracked for internal systems and infrastructure and provide a recent copy of such reports.
- Please provide copies of all IT policies and procedures (development process, security [both physical and electronic], backup and recovery, data privacy, trade secret policies, Acceptable Use Policies, regulatory compliance, export control, internal controls, etc.).

Miscellaneous

Are there any other documents or pieces of information that the Company views as material to operation of the business that weren't covered in previous questions? If so, please provide them.

A BIG THANK YOU

Apparently writing a book is hard. Who knew? I owe a big thank you to the following people:

Emily Holdman: The woman is an organizing, project-managing, editing, and negotiating beast. I know you're not supposed to call women "beasts," but that's the best description. Emily, in all seriousness, thank you.

Susanne Bylund: Thanks for keeping me out of the ditch. You're always pessimistically two steps behind and optimistically three steps ahead.

Mike Dariano, Clayton Dorge, Connor Leonard, Eric Jorgenson, George Odden, Graham Lloyd, Ian Cassel, Jeff Anello, Jeff Gramm, Jenny Heller, John Garrett, Jordan Geotas, Kelie Morgan, Khe Hy, Kyle Eschenroeder, Mills Snell, Morgan Housel, Nate Broughton, Patrick O'Shaughnessy, Peter Racen, Rohit Nagpal, Santi Montoya, Sejal Patel, Savneet Singh, Shane Parrish, Ted Seides: I asked some of the smartest people I know to read through the book and provide feedback. These people spent endless hours editing, commenting, suggesting, and ultimately making the book exponentially better. Thank you all.

Thanks to my parents, Sharon and Lance, for modeling a love of learning, hard work, and selflessness. I only wish more of it had stuck.

Thanks to my girls, Erica, Hattie, Audrey, and Blaise, for putting up with my crazy ideas, relentless travel, and outrageously early bedtime. I love you more than you'll ever know.

CPSIA information can be obtained
at www.ICGtesting.com
Printed in the USA
BVHW020718170720
583884BV00014B/300

9 780998 030005